Chinese Views of Big Data Analytics

DEREK GROSSMAN, CHRISTIAN CURRIDEN, LOGAN MA,
LINDSEY POLLEY, J.D. WILLIAMS, CORTEZ A. COOPER III

Approved for public release; distribution unlimited

RAND NATIONAL DEFENSE RESEARCH INSTITUTE

For more information on this publication, visit www.rand.org/t/RRA176-1

Library of Congress Cataloging-in-Publication Data is available for this publication.
ISBN: 978-1-9774-0476-3

Published by the RAND Corporation, Santa Monica, Calif.
© Copyright 2020 RAND Corporation
RAND® is a registered trademark.

Cover: AdobeStock/daboost; mehaniq41.

Support RAND
Make a tax-deductible charitable contribution at
www.rand.org/giving/contribute

www.rand.org

Preface

China's quest to achieve an artificial intelligence capability to perform a variety of civilian and military functions starts with mastering *big data analytics*—the use of computers to make sense of large data sets. This report provides preliminary analysis of China's expectations for the use of big data analytics and its plans and strategies for the development of big data analytic capabilities, the governmental agencies involved, and some of the particular big data applications it is pursuing. This report is intended to provide an initial baseline description of China's efforts in this area and identify areas for further in-depth research. The report leverages Chinese primary-source materials to understand the current state of Beijing's national big data strategy and the implications of this strategy.

This research was sponsored by the U.S. government and conducted within the Cyber and Intelligence Policy Center of the RAND National Security Research Division, which operates the National Defense Research Institute (NDRI), a federally funded research and development center sponsored by the Office of the Secretary of Defense, the Joint Staff, the Unified Combatant Commands, the Navy, the Marine Corps, the defense agencies, and the defense intelligence enterprise.

For more information on the RAND Cyber and Intelligence Policy Center, see www.rand.org/nsrd/intel or contact the director (contact information is provided on the webpage).

Contents

Summary

China's quest to achieve an artificial intelligence (AI) capability to perform a variety of civilian and military functions starts with mastering *big data analytics*—the use of computers to make sense of large data sets. Our research indicates that China is aggressively working toward becoming a global leader in big data analytics. During the 19th National Congress of the Chinese Communist Party in October 2017, Chinese President Xi Jinping emphasized the need to "promote the deepened integration of Internet, big data, and artificial intelligence with the real economy."[1]

Beijing's efforts are guided by a national big data strategy, an effort that encompasses economic, military, police, and intelligence functions. The 2015 "Action plan for promoting the development of big data" by the State Council of the People's Republic of China partially described China's overall approach to development and utilization of big data analytics. Other agencies with significant big data efforts include the Ministry of Industry and Information Technology, National Development and Reform Commission, Ministry of Education, Ministry of Public Security, People's Liberation Army (PLA), and Ministry of Science and Technology. Our research, informed primarily by Chinese primary-source materials, indicates that Beijing is pursuing the employment of big data to help China achieve great power status.

---

[1] "Full Text of Xi Jinping's Report at the 19th CPC National Congress," Xinhua, November 3, 2017.

In addition to analyzing these primary-source materials, we assessed specific ministry-level plans and guidance from the Ministry of Industry and Information Technology; examined state-run media summaries of Chinese employment of big data analytics; surveyed lesser-known official and semiofficial Chinese publications and discussions, such as those appearing in academic journals and in editorials; reviewed relevant Western publications that cover China's theoretical and practical interests in big data analytics; and queried RAND researchers with deep expertise on the future of computing to help us chart the potential directions Beijing might follow as it presses forward with big data analytics and AI. This analysis led us to identify and focus on two clear priority areas for China's civil and military leaders: Beijing's use of big data analytics in the surveillance of its domestic population, and its use to enhance its military capabilities.

In the domestic arena, the Chinese Communist Party's objective is to leverage big data analytic capabilities to strictly and comprehensively monitor and control China's population. China's public security forces have perhaps been the most enthusiastic to adopt big data analytics. In the absence of laws that limit the collection of data for public security, such powerful tools significantly enhance the Ministry of Public Security's ability to quickly cross-reference criminal records with virtually any other data considered relevant to apprehending alleged criminals. Moreover, improvements in big data analytics directly support the strict monitoring and control of Chinese citizens—including, and perhaps more severely, ethnic minorities—for any signs of perceived disloyalty or other transgressions. The national Social Credit System—an online reputational system that enables or prevents citizens from accessing societal benefits based on their government-rated behavior—is slated to come online by 2020. China is attempting to build a national-level big data system that has the ability to literally prevent crime and political dissent before it ever happens. Beijing would do this by monitoring the habits, associations, and sentiments of every member of society to assess each person's propensity to engage in such activity.

In the military domain, Beijing has shown particular interest in using big data—and, ultimately, AI—to improve a wide variety of

PLA capabilities. China's PLA hopes to have mastered using national defense big data sufficiently to control—or even dominate—the informationized warfare environment, in which control of information is key against great powers. Some of the main areas of interest for application of big data within the military include command, control, communications, computers, intelligence, surveillance, and reconnaissance; equipment and maintenance; logistics; health care; mobilization; training; recruitment; modeling and simulation; and cybersecurity. The use of national defense big data also undergirds Beijing's longer-term effort, which President Xi articulated in his 19th Party Congress speech, to ultimately become the global center for AI by 2030.[2]

Further research into the following questions would provide greater insight into Chinese involvement and investment in big data analytics:

- How might China wield its evolving big data capabilities to monitor and control its population?
- How does China's evolving big data analytic capability rank in comparison with that of the United States in the military domain?
- How is China leveraging big data analysis in support of its research and development processes?
- How does China assess technological or economic trends using big data analytics?
- How does Chinese leadership think about big data–enabled government services and their implications for domestic stability?

---

2 "Full Text of Xi Jinping's Report at the 19th CPC National Congress," 2017.

Acknowledgments

We wish to thank our sponsors in the U.S. government for their leadership in efforts to develop deeper understanding of Chinese approaches to artificial intelligence and big data analytics. We would also like to thank our reviewers and RAND Corporation colleagues Timothy R. Heath and Larry Harrison for their thoughtful comments. Finally, we would like to thank Richard S. Girven and Sina Beaghley of the RAND Cyber and Intelligence Policy Center for their support and guidance.

Abbreviations

AI	artificial intelligence
C4ISR	command, control, communications, computer, intelligence, surveillance, and reconnaissance
CCP	Chinese Communist Party
EM	electromagnetic
IJOP	Integrated Joint Operations Platform
MIIT	Ministry of Industry and Information Technology
MPS	Ministry of Public Security
NDRC	National Development and Reform Commission
OPM	U.S. Office of Personnel Management
PGIS	Police Geographic Information System
PLA	People's Liberation Army
PLAAF	People's Liberation Army Air Force
PLAN	People's Liberation Army Navy
PLASSF	People's Liberation Army Strategic Support Force
R&D	research and development

CHAPTER ONE

Introduction

China's top leaders often express the view that continued economic and military growth is inextricably linked to acquiring or indigenously developing advanced technologies. In virtually every scientific or technological field that can be named—whether robotics, genetics, space technology, drones, nanotechnology, pharmaceuticals, microprocessing, or solar power—China is consistently ranked at or near the top of global leadership. Beijing, however, recognizes that the value of possessing advanced technology alone is limited. Thus, China seeks ways to interconnect and feed its advanced technologies with data—in a system-of-systems approach—to unlock the technologies' full potential.[1]

The next and perhaps ultimate step will be to evolve and infuse computer-aided decisionmaking—commonly known as artificial intelligence (AI)—in a wide variety of governmental, economic, and military applications.[2] Indeed, in the past two years, China's interest in AI technologies has taken center stage.[3] In July 2017, the State Council announced that China "aims to keep pace with the leading coun-

---

[1] For more on this topic, see Jeffrey Engstrom, *Systems Confrontation and System Destruction Warfare: How the Chinese People's Liberation Army Seeks to Wage Modern Warfare*, Santa Monica, Calif.: RAND Corporation, RR-1708-OSD, 2018.

[2] Of course, there is no universal definition of *AI*, but computer-led decisionmaking is the most commonly accepted. For more, see Kelley M. Sayler, *Artificial Intelligence and National Security*, Washington, D.C.: Congressional Research Service, R45178, updated November 21, 2019.

[3] For more on China's recent focus on AI, see Graham Webster, Rogier Creemers, Paul Triolo, and Elsa Kania, "China's Plan to 'Lead' in AI: Purpose, Prospects, and Problems," New America, blog post, August 1, 2017.

tries in AI technology and applications in general by 2020." Moreover, China planned to become "a major center for AI innovation, leading the world in AI technology and applications by 2030."[4]

To become a global center for AI, China must first perfect an intermediary and key enabling step called big data analytics. According to IBM, *big data analytics* is the process by which computers assess large data sets to allow humans (not computers, which is AI) to "gain new insights resulting in better and faster decisions." Big data analytics includes such capabilities as "text analytics, machine learning, predictive analytics, data mining, statistics, and natural language processing."[5]

Our research found that China is aggressively working toward becoming a global leader in big data analytics. During the 19th Party Congress in October 2017, Chinese President Xi Jinping said that China needed to "promote the deepened integration of Internet, big data, and artificial intelligence with the real economy."[6] China has translated *big data* most commonly as 大数据 (*da shuju*)—a term that not only stays true to the literal word-for-word translation of the English term, but retains the same meaning in the Chinese system. Discussions in Chinese primary-source materials confirm that the concept of big data is virtually the same in China as it is in the United States. And, similar to usage in the West, the terms *big data* and *AI* (人工智能, *rengong zhineng*) are sometimes used interchangeably, suggesting that confusion over their precise definitions might likewise exist in the Chinese system, although statements from the highest levels, such as that of Xi cited previously, indicate that Chinese leadership does understand the distinction.

---

[4] "China Maps Out AI Development Plan," Xinhua, July 20, 2017. Also see "New Generation Artificial Intelligence Development Plan [新一代人工智能发展规划]," State Council, July 20, 2017.

[5] IBM, "Big Data Analytics," webpage, undated. Big data analytic techniques can be divided into seven key areas: association rule learning, classification tree analysis, genetic algorithms, machine learning, regression analysis, sentiment analysis, and social network analysis. For more, see Preet Navdeep, Manish Arora, and Neeraj Sharma, "Role of Big Data Analytics in Analyzing e-Governance Projects," *Gian Jyoti e-Journal*, Vol. 6, No. 2, April–June 2016.

[6] "Full Text of Xi Jinping's Report at the 19th CPC National Congress," Xinhua, 2017.

The purpose of this report is to identify and evaluate Chinese expectations for big data analytics. What specifically do the Chinese seek to achieve? What do they believe is within the realm of possibility? Additionally, in which sectors of their society do they plan to apply big data analytics? Our research indicates a variety of activities that Beijing hopes will benefit from big data applications. For this report, we examined two case studies that were selected by our sponsor. The first is a look at China's application of big data analytics to prevent crime or, more cynically, to monitor and control its domestic population. The second examines Beijing's plans to improve the People's Liberation Army's (PLA's) battlespace awareness and targeting operations through big data analytics. We also identified additional case studies for future research, such as big data's implications for China's research and development (R&D) practices, intelligence and counterintelligence operations, or delivery of government services to the people.

Sources and Methods

We focused our research and analysis on Chinese primary-source materials. These included high-level strategic plans and guidance documents, such as the 2015 "State Council action plan for promoting the development of big data [促进大数据发展行动纲要]" and the National Development and Reform Commission's (NDRC's) "List of 2018 Internet+, AI, and Digital Economy Experiments Major Projects Recipients."[7] We also assessed specific ministry-level plans and guidance from the Ministry of Industry and Information Technology (MIIT). In addition, we examined summaries from state-run media—such as *People's Liberation Army Daily* (解放军报)—of Chinese employment of big data analytics. We also surveyed lesser-known official and semiofficial sources of information, such as the PLA's *Whole Military Arms and Equipment Procurement Information Network* [全军武器装备采购信息

---

7 NDRC, "List of 2018 Internet +, AI, and Digital Economy Experiments Major Projects Recipients [2018年"互联网+"、人工智能创新发展和数字经济试点重大工程拟支持项目名单公示]," December 27, 2017.

⺲]. We also drew on unofficial Chinese publications and discussions, particularly those appearing in academic journals and as editorials in the literature. Our focus on Chinese primary sources did not, however, exclude consideration of relevant Western publications that cover China's theoretical and practical interests in big data analytics. Finally, we leveraged RAND Corporation researchers with deep expertise on the future of computing to help us chart the potential directions that Beijing might follow as it presses forward with big data analytics and AI.

Organization of This Report

In Chapter Two, we take a closer look at Chinese leadership guidance on big data analytics and the agencies, industries, and corporations that are involved in this area. We identify projects or initiatives that are underway and the major expected outputs of these efforts. In Chapter Three, we address the first case study on how China is employing or seeks to employ big data analytics for internal safety and security and to monitor and control its population. In Chapter Four, we examine our second case study on the potential utility of big data analytics for the PLA. Chapter Five offers concluding thoughts and highlights areas that might benefit from additional research and analysis.

CHAPTER TWO

China Prioritizing Big Data Analytics

During his marathon speech at the 19th Party Congress in October 2017, President Xi declared that China needs to "promote the deepened integration of Internet, big data, and artificial intelligence with the real economy."[1] With this statement and in numerous pronouncements since, Xi very prominently signaled the emphasis that China puts on achieving an advanced big data analytic capability. Furthermore, by mentioning big data and AI in the same sentence, Xi underscored the close association between these concepts in the Chinese mindset and how the combination of the two will power China toward an AI-driven society by 2030. Viewed through a historical lens, Xi's statement is also the culmination of the past few years of top-level strategic plans and guidance on the need to develop China's big data analytic capability. In this chapter, we take a closer look at the details of these documents and highlight several of the major big data initiatives currently underway and their expected outputs. We also examine the different Chinese state agencies involved in big data analytics.

Implementing the National Big Data Strategy

In December 2017, Xi chaired the second collective study session of the Central Politburo of the Chinese Communist Party (CCP), and the topic was implementation of Beijing's "national big data strategy."

---

[1] "Full Text of Xi Jinping's Report at the 19th CPC National Congress," 2017.

At this session, Xi said that China should "strive to take the initiative to deepen the understanding of the current status and trend of big data development and its impact on economic and social development."[2] Later in the speech, Xi clarified *social development* to mean that China should "improve people's lives" using big data. Xi further argued that "we must make the most use of the big data platform to comprehensively analyze risk factors so as to improve the capability of perceiving, predicting, and preventing those risk factors." Although we could not find a single document that definitively equates to a national strategy for big data, Xi's comments clearly indicate that China has a unified approach to achieving its objectives in this area. The key theme appears to be that, as the technology improves, Beijing will increasingly employ computer-driven trend analyses over human analyses to maximize the efficiency of state-run activities. Key components of the Chinese strategy appear in the plans discussed in this chapter.

Stakeholders in the National Big Data Strategy

Before AI took center stage, in 2017, there was a flurry of activity on big data strategy—particularly from 2014 to 2015. Entities involved included the State Council and MIIT. Additionally, in 2018, the NDRC announced government support for specific big data–related projects, and the Ministry of Education instructed subordinate institutions to prepare for training the future AI workforce. Although we know that China's Ministry of Public Security (MPS) and the PLA are leveraging big data analytics to carry out their missions, we could not find any guidance documents on big data or big data analytics from these agencies. Certainly, other state-run organizations and committees are involved in implementing China's national big data strategy, including, for example, the Ministry of Science and Technology, but

---

[2] "China: Xi Jinping Chairs Second Collective Study Session of Politburo on National Big Data Strategy," Xinhua, December 9, 2017. Summaries can be found at "China Must Accelerate Implementation of Big Data Strategy: Xi," Xinhua, CHR2017120927141422, December 9, 2017.

we could not find substantive information about other agencies participating in the strategy implementation.

The State Council

In 2015, China's State Council issued its "Action Plan for Promoting the Development of Big Data."[3] According to the plan, China has an advantage in big data and should use it to create new platforms for data-sharing with the public and to enhance the government's ability to deliver services to the people. The State Council action plan, for instance, calls for the establishment of databases on China's population, corporations and work units, natural resources, and geography by 2018. Although we could not assess progress across all areas, we found that significant advances have been made in integrating and presenting geographic data.[4] Through the action plan, Beijing has also sought to create joint medical information data systems; an education management platform; and a transportation and tourism database that integrates transportation, public security, weather, earthquake, and geographic data.

The State Council further directed every government at the city level and above to implement a government affairs and public service application with the intent of leveraging these new systems to improve the rule of law, reduce corruption, and enhance risk management. The council specifically called for the creation of mechanisms to track economic data, including financing, taxes, audits, consumption, investment, imports and exports, construction, employment, income distribution, the state of electric power and industry, product quality and safety, and energy saving. The State Council said that it envisions building smart cities that will constantly collect data on China's citizens to improve services and, more nefariously, to monitor and control them.

The State Council also instructed subordinate organizations to examine key data trends in the agricultural sector. The council wants

---

3   State Council, "Action Plan for Promoting the Development of Big Data [促进大数据发展行动纲要]," August 31, 2015.

4   See, for example, Central People's Government [中华人民共和国中央人民政府], "Our Nation Will Build a "Unified Picture" Government Affairs Geographic Information Big Data System [我国将建设政务地理信息大数据 "一张图"]," December 26, 2017.

to use big data analytics to monitor production, consumption, storage, imports and exports, price, cost data for farming products, and other measures on the health of the agricultural sector. This is noteworthy because of the high level of sensitivity surrounding agriculture in China. Chinese leaders have historically faced threats to their continued rule from social unrest in rural areas, putting a premium on being able to prevent and eliminate this type of disruption in the modern era.

Related to its plan for exploiting big data is the State Council's separate 2017 plan for AI, "New Generation Artificial Intelligence Development Plan [新一代人工智能发展规划]." The plan noted that AI was the new focal point for international competition and that achieving advantage in this technology is crucial to maintain national competitiveness and security. The council stated that China must build basic AI infrastructure—including improvements in big data infrastructure—a move that demonstrates that Beijing sees big data as an essential building block to achieving its AI objectives by 2030.

The Ministry of Industry and Information Technology

In 2016, MIIT published its own plan on big data, "Ministry of Industry and Information Technology Big Data Industry Development Plan (2016–2020)."[5] MIIT predicted that, between 2016 and 2020, the income generated by big data products and services would reach $160 billion for the Chinese big data industry, including both private sector and state-owned enterprises, growing at about 30 percent per year. MIIT focused primarily on centralizing Chinese data sets, stating that it would create a national data center for societal management, improving government, and raising people's livelihoods.

MIIT also noted that the government would help big data companies through public-private partnerships to get financing and encourage merger and acquisition activity. MIIT encouraged smart manufacturing, as well as data sharing among telecom, internet, finance, industrial, public transit, and health companies. Of crucial signifi-

---

5   MIIT, "Ministry of Industry and Information Technology Big Data Industry Development Plan (2016–2020) [工业和信息化部关于印发大数据产业发展规划 (2016－2020年)]," December 18, 2016.

cance was MIIT's call for standardizing data quality to facilitate effective sharing of data between Chinese big data organizations.

The National Development and Reform Commission

According to its website, NDRC's primary mission is "to formulate and implement strategies of national economic and social development, annual plans, medium and long-term development plans," which it then submits to the National People's Congress "on behalf of the State Council."[6] In 2017, the NDRC released its comprehensive list of awarded big data projects in its "List of 2018 Internet+, AI, and Digital Economy Experiments Major Projects Recipients."[7] Within this listing were six projects on shipping and logistics, five on facial recognition, five on cloud computing, four on trade, two on natural language processing, two on health data–sharing, and one to build a service platform for China's energy production sources. We expect NDRC's awardees to play a significant role in China's emerging big data and AI landscape.

The Ministry of Education

The State Council's action plan for big data has prompted other Chinese government agencies (such as the Ministry of Education) to issue their own guidance to subordinates to carry out the plan. In April 2018, the ministry published "Ministry of Education Issues and Distributes the Artificial Intelligence Innovation Action Plan for Colleges and Universities."[8] The guidance pressed educational institutions to "promote the research of fundamental theories in fields such as big data intelligence." Furthermore, the ministry sought to "encourage adjustments and integration among such academic fields as artificial intelligence science and technology . . . data science, [and] big data technology." The guidance also designated several key areas of study in big data analytics, including in health, urban planning, and financial

---

6   NDRC, "Main Functions of the NDRC," undated.

7   National Reform and Development Commission, 2017.

8   Ministry of Education, "Ministry of Education Issues and Distributes the Artificial Intelligence Innovation Action Plan for Colleges and Universities [教育部印发《高等学校人工智能创新行动计划]," April 15, 2018.

flows, with an emphasis on big data–driven visual analysis. According to the ministry, big data analysis is already part of the training curriculum at Chinese vocational schools, underscoring the high level of importance Beijing places on properly training its workforce to conduct these activities.

A True Whole-of-Government Approach

Our research demonstrates that China's national big data strategy incorporates several Chinese state-run organizations—making this strategy, similar to that for AI, a truly whole-of-government effort. The leads of the strategy appear to be the State Council, NDRC, and MIIT, possibly in that rank order. Other organizations, such as the Ministry of Education, are supporting the national big data strategy in their own domains. Certainly, many other state organizations play a role in the national big data strategy. The MPS and PLA, in particular, have deep interests in big data to enhance their operations. We turn to these organizations next.

CHAPTER THREE

Case Study I: Preventing Crime and Enhancing Domestic Control

China's public security forces have perhaps been the most enthusiastic to adopt big data analytics. In the absence of legal restrictions on the government's use of personal data for public security, such powerful tools significantly enhance the MPS's ability to quickly cross-reference criminal records with virtually any other data considered relevant to apprehending alleged criminals.[1] Moreover, improvements in big data analytics directly support the strict monitoring and control of Chinese citizens—including, and possibly more severely, ethnic minorities—for any signs of perceived disloyalty or other transgressions. This capability is of great interest to the CCP, so we should expect sustained focus on ensuring that not only the MPS but also other security and intelligence organizations are expanding their employment of these new tools. By the end of 2020, the government plans to integrate all big data–derived monitoring and control tools into what it has called a national *Social Credit System*—an effort to assign reputational rankings to every individual in the Chinese population. Once online, it will represent an

---

[1] "China: Police 'Big Data' Systems Violate Privacy, Target Dissent," Human Rights Watch, blog post, November 19, 2017. Although the People's Republic of China has recently released relatively stringent privacy protection standards, these contain sizable loopholes for the free collection and use of personal data for national security or public safety purposes. As of October 1, 2018, the standards were available from National Information Security Standardization Technical Committee, "[国家标准GB/T 35273-2017 《信息安全技术 个人信息安全规范》获批发布"], January 24, 2018.

unprecedented and truly Orwellian level of state surveillance through technological means.

A Police Cloud with No Limits

The MPS is exploiting new data sets that it plans to centralize in a "police cloud" (警务云).[2] Eventually accessible to all provincial and municipal police authorities, the police cloud will increase the ease with which police can make connections across disparate databases—including non–crime-related systems, such as housing and employment records—to rapidly identify people, places, and businesses of interest. Because China already has a very robust security infrastructure enabled by technology, particularly video cameras, the next step is for security services to integrate the outputs of these devices to provide a comprehensive surveillance picture. Beijing is already routinely comparing information from these systems with the national identification cards of alleged criminals. Although getting all police units to share information has been challenging, the MPS has held up success stories in Shandong and Jiangsu Provinces to demonstrate the value of these programs.[3]

In the city of Weifang, in Shandong, the police have employed a ubiquitous network of closed-circuit television cameras to acquire images that authorities can employ facial-recognition technology against to build databases capable of identifying and tracking individual people and vehicles.[4] This has enabled the police to find and arrest

---

[2] "Public Security Police Cloud Infrastructure Construction and Design [公安警务云基础建设方案设计]," *Journal of People's Public Security University of China (Science and Technology)* [中国人民公安大学警务信息工程学院], January 2016.

[3] See, for example, Wang Jincheng, "Technological Guidance to Service Actual Combat, Strongly Promoting the Construction and Application of Big Data Policing Cloud Computing Across the Entire Force [王金城——科技引导 服务实战强力推进大数据警务云计算全警建设应用]," *Police Technology*, March 2015.

[4] MPS, "Big Data Thinking Improves Police Innovation in Weifang, Shandong [山东潍坊大数据思维推进治安防控创新升级]," September 22, 2015a; MPS, "Weifang, Shandong, Uses Big Data to Innovate a 3-D Law Enforcement System [山东潍坊运用大数据思维创新立体治安防控体系]," October 7, 2015c. In 2015, the MPS called for an "omnipresent, completely connected, always on and fully controllable" nationwide video surveillance network.

suspects after their faces have been detected in public places. During the Qingdao beer festival, for example, police used facial recognition to identify wanted suspects in the crowd, leading to 25 arrests, and also used the technology to identify and refuse admittance to drug addicts.[5] The technology also has enabled the police to conduct proactive policing by collecting all faces in a given area, such as a crowded marketplace; sending the images to a police data center; and associating the images with people wanted by police.[6] The process of police work has only gotten easier with facial-recognition software. According to one report, the police get a text message daily telling them whether a person of interest is in their area of responsibility.[7] Separately, Weifang's "mobile guardian" and "divine eye" systems can automatically identify any vehicle by its license-plate number or other characteristics within seconds and track its movement. Police used these systems to investigate 100 percent of motorbike theft reports and returned all bikes to their owners.[8] In addition, the police leveraged big data trends to assess crime hotspots and redirect assets accordingly.[9]

Another model of big data–driven police work comes from Jiangsu Province. The police in the city of Suqian in Jiangsu Province have increased their percentage of cases solved by 85.1 percent following their work to integrate data from other police organs into their big data system. They use the Police Geographic Information System (PGIS) to standardize, integrate, and, where possible, geolocate 250 million pieces of data. Following the escape of a murder suspect, they put images of the suspect's face from surveillance cameras into

See Josh Chin and Liza Lin, "China's All-Seeing Surveillance State Is Reading Its Citizens' Faces," *Straits Times*, July 8, 2017.

5   "From Ale to Jail: Facial Recognition Catches Criminals at China Beer Festival," *The Guardian*, September 1, 2017.

6   MPS, 2015c. Also see Paul Mozur, "Inside China's Dystopian Dreams: A.I., Shame and Lots of Cameras," *New York Times*, July 8, 2018.

7   "China: Police 'Big Data' Systems Violate Privacy, Target Dissent," 2017.

8   MPS, 2015a; MPS, 2015c.

9   MPS, "Establishing the Big Data Public Security Concept [建立大数据公共安全理念]," September 28, 2015b.

the PGIS, which was able to find matches and identify his primary areas of activity. Within three hours, police were able to find and arrest the suspect.[10] More broadly, police in Jiangsu have used big data to optimize the deployment of resources to the busiest police stations, thereby improving effectiveness and reducing the burden on the officers in those stations.[11] Police have further created personal device–based apps that enable people to more effectively manage interactions with law enforcement. For example, in Shuyang, a county in Jiangsu Province, citizens interact with the police by paying fines and reporting crimes online. The police, in turn, provide important news, such as traffic-flow updates, to civilians.[12] In one case, the Suqian police department used its PGIS to optimize intersections and better allocate traffic police, reducing traffic stoppages by 39 percent and increasing road transportation capacity by 7.25 percent.[13] These types of interactions can build goodwill between the people and law enforcement. Indeed, this or a similar app that is also available in the city of Hangzhou as well as in Jiangsu and Suqian reportedly has a public approval rating of 99.5 percent.[14]

Beyond the success stories in Shandong and Jiangsu, Chinese primary sources indicate many other anecdotes of big data analytics enabling law enforcement to conduct operations or enable citizens to make better decisions. For example, police in the city of Xiamen, in Fujian Province, caught a mail-fraud ring after they noticed that 26 people with past mail-fraud convictions were renting a house together, had been unemployed for the past six months, and had

---

[10] Zhao Jiaxin [赵家新], Li Yirui [李沂瑞], and Tian Tingjiang [田廷江], "Shuyang, Jiangsu, Uses Big Data to Make Social Management Smarter [江苏宿迁运用大数据提升社会治理智能度]," MPS, November 28, 2016.

[11] Zhao, Li, and Tian, 2016.

[12] Zhao, Li, and Tian, 2016.

[13] Zhao, Li, and Tian, 2016.

[14] MPS, "Hangzhou, Jiangsu, Creates a Revolution in Public Security by Researching a Convenient App [浙江杭州警方研发便民服务APP 用大数据助力公安改革]," May 2, 2016; Zhao, Li, and Tian, 2016.

recently registered a point-of-sale machine.[15] The city used a similar system to integrate various bits of data to identify risky and fraudulent online lending platforms.[16] The city's system uses a web crawler to collect information from media and online sources and flags anomalies, such as an official address and actual place of business being different. It also looks for complaints, legal action, bank account information (cash on hand), and profitability. It uses these indicators to rate financial platforms; platforms with poor ratings are investigated. In the future, such a system might be used to monitor the activity of private-equity firms or stock exchanges.[17] Several other municipalities have begun using big data to track financial crimes, money laundering, and terror funding.[18]

Similar to what police did in Jiangsu Province, the police department in the city of Wuhan in Hubei Province partnered with the Chinese company Alibaba to make a transportation app that made data from traffic cameras publicly available, alleviating traffic congestion. It did this in response to noticing that transportation was one of the top complaints of local citizens online. In Shanghai, unlicensed drivers run a high risk of getting pulled over because police use facial-recognition technology. As of December 2017, approximately 835 drivers

---

[15] Zheng Liang [郑良], "Fujian Uses Big Data to Solve the People's Problems [福建大数据破解民生痛点]," MPS, January 14, 2017.

[16] MPS, "Online P2P Is Even Harder to Govern Than Internet Fraud! Xiamen Anti–Fraud Center Develops New Tool to Manage It [比电信诈骗更难治理的是网贷P2P！厦门市继反诈中心又出大数据监管利器]," January 12, 2017a.

[17] MPS, 2017a.

[18] MPS, "Explanation of the State Council's Guidance Opinions on the Anti–Money Laundering, Anti–Terror Funding, Anti–Tax Evasion System [《国务院办公厅关于完善反洗钱、反恐怖融资、反逃税监管体制机制的意见》政策解读]," September 29, 2017b; MPS, "Press Conference on the State Council's Guidance Opinions on the Anti–Money Laundering, Anti–Terror Funding, Anti–Tax Evasion System [《国务院办公厅关于完善反洗钱、反恐怖融资、反逃税监管体制机制的意见》答记者问]," September 29, 2017c; MPS, "Publication of the State Council's Guidance Opinions on the Anti–Money Laundering, Anti–Terror Funding, Anti–Tax Evasion System [国务院办公厅关于完善反洗钱、反恐怖融资、反逃税监管体制机制的意见》正式印发]," September 29, 2017d; State Council, "Internet Financial Risk Improvement Special Implementation Plan [互联网金融风险专项整治工作实施方案]," December 4, 2016a.

had been caught and penalized since the citywide traffic regulation campaign began in 2016. The same technology has supported police in resolving wrong-way driving and even in more minor offenses, such as jaywalking.[19]

Focus on Ethnic Minorities

As noted earlier, CCP leaders especially distrust certain ethnic minorities. Chinese security services employ all of the big data–driven policing techniques described above, along with additional measures to target these populations in the name of preserving domestic stability. The largest and probably most aggressively targeted minority are the Uighurs, an ethnically Turkic and religiously Muslim group whose members live primarily in China's westernmost Xinjiang Province. According to a February 2018 Human Rights Watch report on predictive policing in Xinjiang, the centerpiece of Chinese surveillance activities in the province is the Integrated Joint Operations Platform (IJOP) [一体化联合作战平台].[20] Human Rights Watch noted that, starting in August 2016, the Xinjiang Bureau of Public Security began implementing IJOP, and an earlier program is complete and operational in Kashgar Prefecture in southwest Xinjiang. IJOP employs facial recognition, infrared cameras, and Wi-Fi sniffers that detect identifying addresses of computers

---

[19] "Facial Recognition Identifies Unlicensed Drivers in Shanghai," Xinhua, December 6, 2017.

[20] "China: Big Data Fuels Crackdown in Minority Region," Human Rights Watch, blog post, February 26, 2018. The sources cited in this section are derived from Human Rights Watch's analysis, but we reconstruct them here in full as translated citations for easy follow-up research. For more on IJOP, see "Secretary of the Public Security Bureau of Luzhou Wang Lujun Visited Li County [巴州公安局王鲁军局长到焉耆县调研]," May 17, 2017. For procurement notices announcing the establishment of IJOP, see, for example, "Hetian Public Security Bureau Public Security Checkpoint Project Single Source Procurement Pre-Winning Public Notice [和田市公安局治安检查站项目单一来源采购预中标公公示公告]," February 6, 2017, and "Yecheng County Public Security Bureau 'Integrated Joint Combat Platform' Second Phase Equipment Project Single Source Procurement Publicity KSYCX (DY) 2017–29 [叶城县公安局"一体化联合作战平台"二期设备项目单一来源采购公示 KSYCX（DY）2017–29号]," August 24, 2017.

and other personal devices to accumulate personal data for analysis.[21] These sensors are placed in areas of high interest—for instance, outside homes of religious figures or near entertainment venues. Human Rights Watch has also reported that Chinese authorities are supplementing these data sets by collecting genetic information, fingerprints, iris scans, and blood types of ethnic minorities.[22]

Physical security checkpoints and *visitor management systems*—systems that check all visitors prior to entering restricted-access communities (communities that only allow approved people to enter)—provide additional data on targets' whereabouts and activities.[23] Chinese security officials supplement these surveillance data with regular in-person interviews to determine their targets' "ideological situation" and to otherwise probe for anything the authorities deem relevant to maintaining domestic stability.[24] Predictive policing has been an intensive focus of People's Public Security University of China, the China Electronics Technology Group Corporation, and the Xinjiang Public Security Bureau Special Investigation Unit. Human Rights Watch

---

[21] See, for example, "Ebin County, Minta County, 'Integrated Joint Combat Platform' Video Surveillance Construction Project Publicity Results [塔城区额敏县 "一体化联合作战平台" 视频监控建设项目成交结果公示]," March 21, 2017. Other sources that Human Rights Watch cites—for example, on facial recognition and Wi-Fi sniffers—had been deleted as of May 8, 2018.

[22] "China: Minority Region Collects DNA from Millions: Private Information Gathered by Police, Under Guise of Public Health Program," Human Rights Watch, blog post, December 13, 2017.

[23] Human Rights Watch's sources on these points have been deleted, and, in the case, of visitor management systems, the system website said "the information you want to view does not exist or has not yet been approved!" [您要查看的信息不存在或者还未通过审批!]. The page has since moved or been removed.

[24] "China: Big Data Fuels Crackdown in Minority Region," 2018. In-person interviews could occur every day by a team called Fang Huiju [访惠聚], whose job is to conduct interviews. See, for example, "2017 'Fang Huiju' Visit Newsletter Issue 5 20160301," [2017师市 "访惠聚" 简报05期–20160301], March 1, 2016. Chinese security services probe for anything "unusual." See, for example, Hetian Town Government, "Hetian Area Emergency Management Work Information Phase 1 [和田地区应急管理工作信息 第1期]," January 6, 2017. The Human Rights Watch assessment has a citation for the statement that IJOP looks into anything "related to stability." However, the Chinese statement to that effect has since been deleted.

found that a police list of at least 75 behavioral indicators now feeds into IJOP, allowing security officials to not only conduct big data analysis but also adjust algorithms using feedback from IJOP.[25] Individuals who exhibit risk factors, such as foreign travel of extensive duration, proactive support for local mosques, abnormal electricity consumption, relationships with other people who exhibit risk factors, or the use of apps that help evade surveillance, are automatically flagged by the system. These individuals can then be subjected to police investigation, extrajudicial detention, or restriction from public spaces.[26]

Documents leaked to the *New York Times* in late 2019 suggest that the CCP is taking an almost epidemiological view, comparing extremism with a virus that must be removed through stringent, open-ended, mandatory reeducation, resulting in the incarceration of thousands of Uighurs and other Muslims in Xinjiang. The documents further suggest that the behavior of both detainees and their families will be evaluated and adjudicated to generate a point score, which will, in turn, determine the duration of their confinement.[27] It is unclear how IJOP or other data-driven methods piloted in Xinjiang will fit into the broader infrastructural framework of the police cloud, although it is possible that many IJOP features will eventually be implemented by police outside Xinjiang.[28]

---

[25] "Identify 75 Religious Extreme Activities [识别75种宗教极端活动]," *Nanchang Gonganju* [南昌公安局], September 8, 2015. For more on Chinese conceptual thinking on algorithms, see "An Anti-Terrorism Risk Analysis Method Based on Bayesian Theory [一种基于贝叶斯理论的反恐风险分析方法]," *China National Knowledge Infrastructure*, September 2017.

[26] "China's Algorithms of Repression: Reverse-Engineering a Xinjiang Police Mass Surveillance App," Human Rights Watch, May 1, 2019.

[27] Austin Ramzy and Chris Buckley, "'Absolutely No Mercy': Leaked Files Expose How China Organized Mass Detentions of Muslims, *New York Times,* November 16, 2019.

[28] "China's Algorithms of Repression: Reverse-Engineering a Xinjiang Police Mass Surveillance App," 2019.

National Social Credit System: Coming Soon

In 2014, the State Council announced that China was pursuing the creation of a national Social Credit System.[29] As mentioned previously, the national Social Credit System is a government effort to assign reputational rankings to every person in the Chinese population. The rankings could be used to prevent low-ranking people from accessing certain societal benefits and to reward high-ranking people with improved access to such benefits. Proposed to come online at some point in 2020, this system will leverage big data analytic techniques already employed by various Chinese companies and municipalities.

The project began when Beijing gave licenses to eight companies to test their algorithms in an effort to see whether these capabilities might be appropriate for the government to use to both protect and control its citizenry. Beijing reportedly relies heavily on Tencent (developer of the popular multipurpose messaging platform WeChat) and Alibaba (a Chinese online purchasing and delivery service, similar to Amazon) as proving grounds for making digital connections across enormous and disparate data sets.[30] Specifically, a credit history scoring group run by Alibaba, known as Sesame Credit, has been at the heart of planning efforts for the Social Credit System. Unlike in the United States, where credit history is evaluated in a vacuum, Sesame Credit and others like it are combining credit history checks with other indicators of "good" or "bad" behavior. This should come as no surprise given that the CCP, from its earliest days, kept dossiers known as *dang'an* (档案) on all individuals to evaluate an individual's trustworthiness and whether political reeducation or another form of punishment was required. From this perspective, the national Social Credit System will essentially be a digitized 21st-century version of the CCP's files on its population.

---

[29] "Planning Outline for the Construction of a Social Credit System (2014–2020)," *China Copyright and Media*, blog post, June 14, 2014, updated April 25, 2015. Also see State Council, "State Council Guidance Principles for the Building of the Social Credit System [国务院办公厅关于加强个人诚信体系建设的指导意见]," December 30, 2016b.

[30] Rachel Botsman, "Big Data Meets Big Brother as China Moves to Rate Its Citizens," *Wired UK*, October 21, 2017.

Sesame Credit has demonstrated techniques for turning personal data into trustworthiness ratings that will likely be at least partially incorporated into the mandatory national Social Credit System in 2020. The new system will work by combining credit history checks with checks across many dozens—perhaps hundreds—of other databases on citizens' activities and lifestyle choices.[31] In Alibaba's Sesame Credit, these databases are organized into four key areas, aside from personal credit history. First, there is "a user's ability to fulfill his/her contract obligations," suggesting that this is a measure of whether someone's employment status and salary data are sufficient to satisfy their responsibilities.[32] Second, all individuals must verify their personal information and characteristics through official surveys. Third, an individual's lifestyle choices are represented by data sets on their purchasing behavior, where and how the individual spends their time, and what the individual says online and elsewhere, and these results are heavily scrutinized. Finally, an individual's associates are also rated, with a corresponding impact on the individual.

Once the system goes online, citizen scores will be made public to convince people to avoid shame through score improvement. Score association provides an obvious incentive to stay away from "bad" people. It appears to be intentionally aimed at splitting groups and therefore preventing them from causing unrest that might threaten CCP regime stability. Under the national Social Credit System, for example, a political dissident who posts negative remarks about the government online will likely become isolated from society because, theoretically, no one will want to lower their score by associating with a low-scoring dissident.[33] To be sure, the political realm is only one of many areas of behavior that can affect a person's score. Individual pur-

---

[31] At least 30 local governments already support the initiative. See "China Invents the Digital Totalitarian State," *The Economist*, December 17, 2016.

[32] Alibaba Group, "Ant Financial Unveils China's First Credit-Scoring System Using Online Data," press release, Hangzhou, China, January 28, 2015.

[33] Rick Falkvinge, "In China, Your Credit Score Is Now Affected by Your Political Opinions—and Your Friends' Political Opinions," *Privacy News Online*, blog post, October 3, 2015.

chases will be highly scrutinized to determine a person's work ethic. Someone who buys diapers might be considered more responsible than someone who buys video games, because the latter can be inferred to indicate youth and laziness.[34] Ultimately, the CCP is looking to gauge the level of trustworthiness of each and every citizen, as defined by the party. The CCP can incentivize "good" scores by offering easier access to credit, rentals without needing a deposit, expedited visas, and preferential access to dating sites. Proposed penalties for lower scores include reduced access to education and housing, difficulties acquiring financing and government funding, and travel restrictions.[35]

The idea of having a "reward system" is not new in communist-ruled China. Each year, Beijing awards hundreds of thousands of people with all kinds of honors, such as "outstanding cadre" or "civilized village," with prizes ranging from money to a higher pension to better health insurance and public housing.[36] Digitizing this system on a massive scale has raised CCP leadership expectations that, by the end of 2020, the regime can rule over a country that truly "allow[s] the trustworthy to roam everywhere under heaven while making it hard for the discredited to take a single step."[37]

It should be noted that this project is not uncontroversial within China. In summer 2019, the government of Wulian County in Shandong Province drew criticism for putting a teacher on the county's social credit blacklist for subjecting students to corporal punishment, with some netizens arguing that creditworthiness should be a purely financial affair. Although the teacher's school took administrative action against him (a relatively uncontroversial consequence for his use of corporal punishment), he was eventually taken off the blacklist, and an article criticizing the decision to blacklist him was reposted on the website of the CCP-run *People's Daily*, indicating a certain level of offi-

---

[34] Botsman, 2017.

[35] "China Invents the Digital Totalitarian State," 2016.

[36] "China Invents the Digital Totalitarian State," 2016.

[37] Amy Hawkins, "Chinese Citizens Want Their Government to Rank Them," *Foreign Policy*, May 24, 2017.

cial support or at least toleration of its views.[38] Similarly, in early 2018, Chinese citizens reacted with outrage when China's Ant Financial began enrolling them in its social credit scheme without their knowledge.[39] As of July 2020, although some companies and local governments continue to experiment with social credit systems, it remains unclear how Beijing will craft its national social credit policy, and to what extent public discontent will restrain it from implementing on a national scale some of the more draconian measures used in Xinjiang.

COVID-19: Dress Rehearsal for Population Control?

In the final days of 2019 and into 2020, the illness caused by a unique strain of coronavirus, COVID-19, raged across China. Once Beijing decided to step in and treat the epidemic as a national emergency, Chinese technology, communications, and transportation companies got involved. Telecom companies (presumably using their access to smart-phone-generated location data) and travel companies began to track people who had traveled to or from places with high infection rates, often publishing lists of these people along with the mode of travel they took so that anyone who had had contact with them could be tested or quarantined.[40] Chinese telecom companies developed a service that allows users to get a report of their location for the past 14 days so that individuals can prove to employers, apartment committees, or others that they had not been to an area where there had been a major outbreak.[41] Both Tencent and Alibaba have designed apps to help people

---

[38] Gao Lu [高路], "Credit Blacklists: Not the Solution to Every Social Problem [信用黑名单，不能啥都往里装]," *Qianjiang Evening News* [钱江晚报], trans. Ryan Soh and Jeffrey Ding for *ChinAI*, No. 61, July 30, 2019.

[39] Paul Mozur, "Internet Users in China Expect to Be Tracked. Now, They Want Privacy," *New York Times*, January 4, 2018. Note that many Chinese users continue to use Ant Financial's apps.

[40] Hu Yong, "The Public Interest and Personal Privacy in a Time of Crisis (Part I)" *Weixin*, trans. Jeff Ding for *ChinAI*, No. 85, March 6, 2020a.

[41] Shawn Yuan, "How China Is Using AI and Big Data to Fight the Coronavirus," *Al Jazeera*, March 1, 2020.

know when they might be at risk for having contracted the virus.[42] Alibaba's Alipay Health Code app, which reportedly uses an AI algorithm to analyze reported symptoms, travel history, and location data to classify users as green, yellow, or red based on their risk of having contracted the disease, has been adopted by at least 100 municipalities, and there are reports of employers, apartment managers, and even police officers at freeway off-ramps refusing access to anyone who does not have a "green" score.[43]

As with the Social Credit System, Chinese efforts to control the population during the pandemic have not been without controversy. Hu Yong, a professor from Peking University's School of Journalism and Communication whose blog has 800,000 followers, has criticized China's response for making more demands on individual rights than necessary, even given the crisis.[44] Many Chinese citizens from Hubei (the province at the epicenter of the pandemic) complained of widespread discrimination, much of which is facilitated by official divulsion of personal information, national identification cards that immediately identify the location of a citizen's official residence, and perhaps even by the Alipay Health Code app.[45] The opaque way in which the app determines a person's risk (which, in turn, could determine whether they can return to their homes or workplaces) has angered some users.[46]

It should be noted that, in the face of this outbreak, China is not the only country curtailing some personal freedoms to prevent infection, and around the world, such moves are often supported by local populations.[47]

---

[42] Pratik Jakhar, "Coronavirus: China's Tech Fights Back," *BBC Monitoring*, March 3, 2020.

[43] Paul Mozur, Raymong Zhong, and Aaron Krolik, "In Coronavirus Fight, China Gives Citizens a Color Code, with Red Flags," *New York Times,* March 1, 2020.

[44] Hu Yong, "The Public Interest and Personal Privacy in a Time of Crisis (Part II)" *Weixin*, trans. Jeff Ding for *ChinAI*, No. 86, March 6, 2020b.

[45] Hu Yong, 2020a; Hu Yong, 2020b; Jakhar, 2020.

[46] Mozur, Zhong, and Krolik, 2020.

[47] Grace Moon, "This Is How South Korea Flattened Its Coronavirus Curve," NBC News, March 24, 2020.

What is potentially concerning about China's response is that the tools the CCP is developing during the crisis—to track its citizens and autonomously restrict their movements using their data—could be deployed later for more-repressive purposes. As noted in previous sections, the Chinese government and Chinese companies (and other companies and governments around the world) have long collected data on people's travel, location, health, and a vast array of other activities. China, however, may be unique in the scale at which it is willing to force employers, telecom companies, police, hospitals, businesses, and local governments to pool their data, and then to mete out restrictions to citizens automatically as a result of those data. As Hu Yong noted, "But you might as well ask yourself: Has history ever shown that once the government has surveillance tools, it will maintain modesty and caution when using them?"[48]

Omniscience with Chinese Characteristics

This section demonstrates that the CCP's objective is to leverage big data analytic capabilities to strictly and comprehensively monitor and control its own population. China is literally building a national-level surveillance and big data system that rivals even the most audacious fictitious accounts depicted in well-known dystopian literature, such as George Orwell's *1984*. Similar to the rating system depicted in *Black Mirror*'s episode "Nosedive" (Series 3, Episode 1, October 2016), the social credit score will, in theory, work to constrain individual action as citizens seek to attain the benefits of high scores and avoid the dangers of low scores.[49] Some of the CCP's most ambitious projects (espe-

---

[48] Hu Yong, 2020b.

[49] Mara Hvistendahl, "Inside China's Vast New Experiment in Social Ranking," *Wired*, December 14, 2017. Although no major media outlet has, as far as we could find, made the connection between *Black Mirror*'s dystopian view and the Social Credit System, some bloggers have made it, although there is disagreement as to how accurate the comparison is with the Chinese system. See, for example, Mianzi Jingxuan, "Are They Approaching Hell? China Will Implement Black Mirror's Scoring System [面子精选], [他人即地狱？中国要实行《黑镜》里的评分制了]," *Sohu*, December 14, 2017.

cially in Xinjiang) are, in some ways, also similar to the "precrime" technology depicted in the 2002 film *Minority Report* (based on Philip K. Dick's 1956 novel of the same name), in which police are able to predict and prevent crimes before they happen. The CCP seems to believe that many crimes can be prevented by collecting as much data as possible on individual citizens, then preemptively surveilling or even arresting those who present certain risk factors. Beijing hopes that such techniques will enable it to stop crime—and political dissent, so "pre-unrest" would be an accurate description here as well—before it ever happens, and to mold its most unruly citizens into more-pliable people.

Beijing is already using these techniques and is adding a new and insidious dimension that incentivizes good behavior through the credit system. Moreover, Beijing appears to place faith in these capabilities to map out areas that are particularly prone to worrisome activities and correspondingly shifts resources to address these problems. Ultimately, Chinese leaders want to build a predictive policing capability to achieve total and complete capacity to control societal interaction.

CHAPTER FOUR

Case Study II: Enhancing People's Liberation Army Warfighting Capabilities

During his 19th Party Congress speech in October 2017, President Xi noted his intent for the PLA to fully transform itself into "world-class forces" by 2050.[1] In support of this long-term objective, China considers big data analytics to be a vital national resource. Beijing has shown particular interest in using big data—and, ultimately, AI—to improve a wide variety of PLA capabilities, which we describe in detail in this chapter. The common theme throughout Chinese primary sources is that mastery of big data analytics will better position China to win future military conflicts between great powers.

Defining Big Data for the People's Liberation Army

Although no comprehensive public document exists on the PLA's designs for big data, a survey of multiple publicly available items suggests an emphasis on big data, in line with achieving national defense prerogatives. One article, published in June 2016, broadly outlined national defense big data (国防大数据).[2] The article's authors defined

---

1   "Full Text of Xi Jinping's Report at the 19th CPC National Congress," 2017.

2   He You [何友], Zhu Yangyong [朱扬勇], Zhao Peng [赵鹏], Chai Yong [柴勇], Liao Zhicheng [廖志成], Zhou Wei[周伟], Zhou Xiangdong [周向东], Wang Haipeng [王海鹏], Wang Wei [汪卫], Xiong Yun [熊赟], Xu Zhoujun [许舟军], Peng Xuan [彭煊], Meng Hui [孟晖], and Wang Shengjin [王生进], "Panorama of National Defense Big Data [系统工程与电子技术]," *Systems Engineering and Electronics* [国防大数据概论], Vol. 6, 2016.

national defense big data as the collective data generated by military activities—such as the defense of national sovereignty, unity, territorial integrity, and security—and data resources generated by political, economic, scientific, diplomatic, education, and other activities that are related to military issues.

Key characteristics of national defense big data go beyond those of general big data (high velocity, high variety, high volume, and high value) to incorporate *6S* characteristics, including supercomplexity [复杂性], supersecrecy [超保密性], speedy deployment [高机动性], safety [高安全性], a strong degree of confrontation [强对抗性], and strong timeliness [强实时性]. *Supercomplexity* means that military data, in many cases, might be more difficult to process than general data. *Supersecrecy* underscores the importance of protecting national defense big data from exfiltration or attack by hostile forces. *Speedy deployment* is defined as being able to flexibly employ military data in multiple domains of warfare on an on-demand basis. *Safety* describes the need to defend the infrastructure that supports big data analysis, such as electricity and computer hardware. *Strong degree of confrontation* notes that achieving a national defense big data capability is a competition that occurs in a noncooperative context. Finally, *strong timeliness* describes an operational environment in which decisionmaking must occur quickly because of an ever-changing battlefield situation.

National Defense Big Data Is Key to Winning the Great Power Struggle

By developing these 6S characteristics, China seeks to bolster its top-line objective to build armed forces capable of "winning informationized local wars" [打赢信息化局部战争].[3] Since the concept first appeared in China's most recent defense white paper, in 2015, it has been widely interpreted to mean fielding a transformed PLA capable of controlling—

---

3   *Winning Informationized Local Wars* [打赢信息化局部战争] is actually the ninth revision of Chinese strategic guidelines [军事战略方针] since the founding of the People's Republic of China. For more on this history, see M. Taylor Fravel, "China's New Military Strategy: 'Winning Informationized Local Wars,'" *China Brief,* Vol. 15, No. 13, July 2, 2015.

and one day dominating—the information warfare environment to successfully win wars in its own region—most notably, in Taiwan and in the East and South China Seas. Indeed, according to multiple Chinese sources, mastery of national defense big data exploitation has become key to winning these types of wars against other advanced states.

For instance, according to Li Daguang at China's National Defense University's Military Logistics and Military Science and Technology Equipment Teaching and Research Department, national defense big data has become a new focal point in the struggle between great powers.[4] Li further opined that data sovereignty in the network space is just as critical as land, sea, air, and space sovereignty. Big data will be an important component of system-of-systems confrontation, which the PLA assesses will be the primary theme of warfare in the 21st century. According to Shang Zelian, director of the Mobilization Department at Nanjing Army Command College,

> systems confrontation and joint operations will produce a large volume of data . . . only by comprehensively, precisely, and rapidly unearthing the crucial points from complex data sources can we effectively organize confrontations, break through the fog of war, and achieve precise design of warfare.[5]

Liu Linshan, a researcher at the PLA Academy of Military Science's Information Research Center, noted that, with the advent of the "Big Data era," national defense big data now plays a decisive role as a "strategic resource."[6] For Liu, the proliferation of big data signals the arrival of a new form of warfare, with data offense and data defense at its core. Victory will be achieved by plundering and destroying enemy data resources while building and utilizing data superiority to rapidly make

---

4   Cheng Rong [程荣] and Pei Xian [裴贤], "National Defense Big Data: The Intelligent Core That Protects National Security   [国防大数据: 守护国家安全的智慧芯]," *People's Liberation Army Daily* [解放军日报], January 11, 2017.

5   Cheng and Pei, 2017.

6   Liu Linshan [刘林山], "What Is the Function of Big Data in the Construction of a Modern National Defense and the Military? [大数据在国防和军队现代化建设中有何作用?]," *People's Liberation Army Daily*, February 1, 2018.

operational decisions leading to success. Data are particularly critical for the conduct of joint operations, according to Liu. Only with the efficient flow of data through data-sharing, integration, and interoperability between various operational elements can the cognitive limitations of commanders be overcome, thus shortening the time needed for precise decisionmaking. Big data is also conducive to more-efficient management of military resources.

We also reviewed Chinese writings on national defense big data at the operational level. Echoing Liu's vision, for example, China's Northern Theater Command commander, Lieutenant General Li Qiaoming, assessed that command decisionmaking should become autonomous by seamlessly leveraging data derived from various units, services, and the battlefield.[7] According to Li, the PLA should employ technology using cloud computing and the Internet of Things. Flat structures, simple and integrated hierarchies, and system integration represent the current developmental direction of operational command systems, which will eventually set the stage for the "intelligentization" [智能化], of warfare. For Beijing, explicit use of the term *intelligentization*, whether in the military or civilian sphere, indicates greater levels of automation. Although most PLA scholars believe that AI will never replace human operational commanders completely, they do believe that it can act as a "digital staff officer" capable of gathering and presenting intelligence on the enemy, identifying enemy intent, and monitoring operations.[8]

One of the more expansive writings on big data's implications for the PLA comes from the deputy commander of the Central Theater Command, Lieutenant General Zhang Xudong.[9] Writing while he was commander of the ground forces in the Central Theater Command, Zhang presented four main points. First, battlefield commanders must clearly understand the new changes brought on by big data. Data

---

[7]   Li Qiaoming [李桥铭], "Big Data: Making War Commanding Decisions More Scientific [大数据: 让战争指挥决策更科学]," *People's Liberation Army Daily*, February 28, 2017.

[8]   Yuan Yi [袁艺], "Will AI Command Future Wars? [人工智能将指挥未来战争？]," *Defense Daily* [中国国防报], January 12, 2017.

[9]   Zhang Xudong [张旭东], "Zhang Xudong: Seize the Initiative in Future Battlefield Data [张旭东: 抢占未来战场数据主导先机]," *People's Liberation Army Daily*, August 31, 2017.

superiority has become a new mechanism for victory in combat, and data-driven decisionmaking has become the new paradigm for combat decisionmaking. Second, commanders must maintain clarity about the overall strategy for building military big data. They must seek to merge civil-military efforts in a concerted manner, broaden channels of big data resources, construct a big data storage system, and boost the quality and effectiveness of big data flow and transmission. Third, commanders must tap into the combat potential for military big data. This includes bringing the superiorities of big data into play by focusing on the opponent and sticking close to frontline requirements. It also means R&D of software specialized for military big data, the construction of powerful big data combat command platforms, and the establishment of big data combat-support forces. Finally, commanders must strengthen the initiative of the use of military big data. Zhang believed that this would entail seizing the initiative on big data employment and striving to become experts on big data, the operation of big data software, and the planning functions of big data.

Military Applications of Big Data

These types of conceptualizations have led the PLA to explore potential opportunities in the application of national defense big data. Some of the main areas of interest include command, control, communications, computers, intelligence, surveillance, and reconnaissance (C4ISR); equipment and maintenance; logistics; health care; mobilization; training; recruitment; modeling and simulation; and cybersecurity.

Basic Big Data Infrastructure

Before the PLA can leverage big data analytics to improve warfighting capabilities, it must first build the requisite big data infrastructure. The PLA therefore plans to significantly strengthen its ability to store, transmit, and analyze national defense big data.[10] Beijing must create a mas-

---

[10] Han Ming [韩明], Yang Jibao [杨继宝], and Lu Xiang [卢祥], "The Era of Big Data War [大数据战时代]," *China New Telecommunications* [中国心通信], Vol. 11, 2017.

sive and "containerized" national defense big data platform, suggesting that the system must have clearly defined infrastructural boundaries and perhaps specific mission sets; this is according to an article produced collaboratively among the Naval Aviation Engineering College Mixed Information Research Institute, the Tsinghua University Department of Electrical Engineering, Fudan University Computer Science College, Beijing Remote Sensing Research Institute, and Beijing Information Technology Research Institute.[11] The authors of that article further argued for an "embedded" concept of national defense big data systems that will enable the PLA to attain the upper hand in future, intelligentized conflicts. In a separate call for bids, the PLA sought to procure data-storage systems with centralized deployment, management, monitoring, and security. Each of these systems would include two management nodes, data nodes, service switches, management switches (as in telecommunications), and all necessary software. Each data node would have 16 gigabytes of storage, and the system would have 40 terabytes of storage.[12] Another article from the China Academy of Electronics and Information Technology argued that a command intelligence system must be able to integrate many different types of battlefield data, as well as publicly available intelligence. Such a system could use Hadoop architecture and tools, such as Hadoop Storm and Hadoop Spark, to gather, store, and manipulate large amounts of data. It would serve a variety of military customers, from combined command centers down to individual soldiers.[13] Of note, the PLA Air Force (PLAAF) Early Warning Academy has also

---

[11] He You et al., 2016.

[12] "Big Data Machine [大数据一体机]," *Whole Military Weapons and Equipment Purchase Information Net* [全军武器装备采购信息网], April 5, 2016.

[13] Guo Jiguang [郭继光] and Huang Sheng [黄胜], "Study on Architecture of Big Data Based on Military Intelligence Analysis and Service System [基于大数据的军事情报分析与服务系统架构研究]," *Journal of the Chinese Academy of Electronics and Information Technology* [中国电子科学研究院学报], Vol. 4, 2017.

been doing work on improving Hadoop scheduling methods for intelligence analysis, and the People's Armed Police seems interested as well.[14]

Beijing, however, recognizes that building national defense big data infrastructure alone will be insufficient because it needs human talent to manage and operate these systems. For example, according to the Equipment College's Complicated Electrical Systems Simulation Laboratory, many people talk about modeling and big data but do not actually understand the mechanisms that connect them. Thus, the Equipment College sought to lay out two "bridge" theories, presumably to connect the two.[15] Meanwhile, an editorial stated that the PLA must work to perfect its big data regulations and recruit more people skilled in big data.[16]

Command, Control, Communications, Computers, Intelligence, Surveillance, and Reconnaissance

The PLA overall, and especially the PLA Navy (PLAN) and PLAAF, is clearly interested in both using national defense big data to integrate output from multiple sensors of different types and to leverage deep learning to identify recognizable characteristics of targets to improve and automate target differentiation. This data integration should enable PLA commanders to have a clearer picture of the battlefield and to confidently identify distant targets despite fragmentary information. Big data and AI projects have been commissioned to analyze

---

[14] Jiang Surong [蒋苏蓉] and Meng Jiangqiao [蓝江桥], "Timeout Prediction of the Schedule Method for Big Data of the Intelligence Analysis Based on Hadoop [Hadoop框架下的情报分析大数据调度超时预测方法]," *Computer Science* [计算机科学], Supp. 1, 2014; Li Chongdong [李崇东], "Study on the Construction of the Military Decision-Making System Based on Large Data Support [基于大数据支持的军事决策系统构建研究]," *Software Engineering* [软件工程], Vol. 3, 2016.

[15] Wang Shoubiao [王寿彪], Li Xinming [李新明], and Liu Dong [刘东], "Concept Association Mechanisms and Model Structures on Equipment System of Systems with Big Data [大数据与装备体系的概念关联机理和模型结构]," *Journal of the Chinese Academy of Electronics and Information Technology* [中国电子科学研究院学报], Vol. 5, 2016.

[16] Fu Zhong-li [傅中力], Zhuang Huang [张煌], and Li Po [李坡], "National Security and Military Strategy Selection in an Era of Big Data [大数据时代的国家安全与军事战略选择]," *National Defense Science and Technology*, Vol. 2, 2013.

input from satellite, visual light, radar, infrared, sonar, and other sensors, as well as publicly available intelligence.

The most ambitious of these projects aimed to integrate data from multiple sensor types to locate and identify targets. Specifically, the project sought to use online satellite images as a data set and integrate at least five forms of data: online shipping data (including text), high-resolution or multispectral cameras, infrared, synthetic aperture radar, and electromagnetic (EM) emission information to automatically find and track ships. The system should identify ship location with 85-percent accuracy and track ship navigation paths with 80-percent accuracy.[17] Another plan called for building a prototype program that could automatically integrate fragmentary data from shore-, sea-, air-, and space-based radars; photoelectric sensors; other sensors; and human intelligence sources to identify targets in middle to far seas.[18] Big data historical analysis is also important to target identification for the PLA. For example, a Western Theater Command PLAAF radar brigade used an analytic database system to compare characteristics of unidentified

---

[17] "Naval Research: Satellite Data Mining Technology Based on Big Data [海军预研–基于大数据的卫星信息数据挖掘技术]," *Whole Military Weapons and Equipment Purchase Information Net* [全军武器装备采购信息网], August 1, 2016. For a similar but apparently unfunded proposal from 2016, see "Using Big Data and Machine Learning to Analyze and Forecast from Multiple Information Sources–315020301 [信息系统–315020301–大数据背景下基于深度学习的多源情报分析与预测技术]," *Whole Military Weapons and Equipment Purchase Information Net* [全军武器装备采购信息网], August 28, 2016. This system was slated to be capable of tracking changes in the battlefield and the enemy's intent and predicting a target's changes and movements. It was going to use at least six methods for identifying target patterns, four methods of gathering target information, four algorithms for target information integration, three methods to assist in targeting, and three methods for battlefield visualization.

[18] "Naval Innovation—30201050404—Technology to Provide Information on Targets in the Middle and Far Seas with Big Data [海军创新–30201050404–基于大数据的中远海海上目标信息处理技术]," *Whole Military Weapons and Equipment Purchase Information Net* [全军武器装备采购信息网], April 25, 2017. For another, possibly related project, see "Naval Advanced Research—Ship Big Data Mining and Processing Technology [海军预研–船舶大数据挖掘与处理技术]," *Whole Military Weapons and Equipment Purchase Information Net* [全军武器装备采购信息网], August 14, 2016.

air activity with those in similar cases from the past, allowing for rapid identification of unidentified aircraft.[19]

There are many other examples of the PLA pursuing big data–enabled or big data–enhanced C4ISR projects. According to one Chinese notice, the PLA plans to build a system that uses machine learning on a large library of infrared images, visual images, and 25-frame-per-second video images of warships and civilian vessels to create a method that distinguishes between them with 95-percent accuracy.[20] In another project, the PLAN aims to use images from all remote sensors to create an image database on which to train deep learning algorithms to differentiate between different types of warships, then use those algorithms to build a multi-sensor warship detection platform.[21] Under ideal conditions, a camera with a resolution of 2.5 meters should be able to identify medium-sized warships with 95 percent accuracy and only 10 percent false positives. If resolution is ten to 16 meters, the platform should be able to identify large warships (aircraft carriers) with 90 percent accuracy and 15 percent false positives. According to the details of one such related project synopsis, the PLA sought to build aircraft-mounted multisensor and multispectrum systems to differentiate between soil, rock, water, and synthetic objects with 90 percent accuracy.[22] In another project synopsis, we found that the PLA has started a small patent study on the state of computer vision, superhu-

[19] Jia Chong [贾冲], "Databases, Assisting High-Quality and Rapid Support [数据库, 助保障优质快速]," *Air Force Daily*, May 27, 2016.

[20] "Naval Innovation—30201050111—Image Processing and Ship Target Recognition Based on Artificial Intelligence [海军创新-30201050111-基于人工智能的图像处理和舰船目标识别技术]," *Whole Military Weapons and Equipment Purchase Information Net* [全军武器装备采购信息网], March 31, 2017.

[21] "Naval Innovation—30201050110—Marine Remote Sensing Target Information Mining Technology Based on Deep Learning [海军创新-30201050110-基于深度学习的海洋遥感目标信息挖掘技术]," *Whole Military Weapons and Equipment Purchase Information Net*, March 31, 2017.

[22] "Key Laboratory Fund—6142A010103—New Model of Spectral Matching for Ground Objects Supported by Multisource Remote Sensing Big Data [重点实验室基金-6142A010103-多源遥感大数据支持下的地物光谱匹配新模型研究]," *Whole Military Weapons and Equipment Purchase Information Net* [全军武器装备采购信息网], May 19, 2017.

man visual perception and tracking, online image and video analysis, and three-dimensional re-creation from images.[23]

The PLA is also pursuing big data analytic capabilities to differentiate military signals. In one example, the PLA sought to use partially supervised learning to identify the characteristics of different types of EM signals, such as those from communications equipment, radar, and navigation systems. This system would be able to identify characteristics of a signal (and presumably thus identify it) within 0.1 seconds and to model the signals it receives within 10 seconds.[24] In the area of target identification, the PLA is attempting to develop technology that performs high-quality differentiation of synthetic aperture radar images by using machine learning to identify target characteristics.[25] A separate project planned to use deep learning to create a method that uses multiple photoelectric sources to identify a target's characteristics (presumably for target identification and differentiation) and movements.[26] The PLA further sought to employ deep learning to enhance target distinguishing with radar, particularly as the target changes form or imperfect historical target data are available.[27] Similarly, in the undersea domain, the PLAN is interested in developing technology that will

---

[23] "Artificial Intelligence Series 3—Patent Analysis of Key Technologies in Computer Vision [人工智能系列3—计算机视觉关键技术专利分析]," *Whole Military Weapons and Equipment Purchase Information Net* [全军武器装备采购信息网], December 23, 2017.

[24] "Fund—61401370502—Research on Signal Feature Extraction Based on Deep Learning [基金-61401370502-基于深度学习的信号特征提取技术研究]," *Whole Military Weapons and Equipment Purchase Information Net* [全军武器装备采购信息网], August 1, 2016.

[25] "Key Laboratory Fund—61425030202—Microwave Imaging Automatic Recognition Technology [重点实验室基金-61425030202-微波成像自动识别技术]," *Whole Military Weapons and Equipment Purchase Information Net* [全军武器装备采购信息网], May 19, 2017.

[26] "Key Laboratory Fund—61421070104—Optical Information Fusion Technology Based on Big Data [重点实验室基金-61421070104-基于大数据的光电信息融合技术]," *Whole Military Weapons and Equipment Purchase Information Net* [全军武器装备采购信息网], May 19, 2017.

[27] "Fund—61404130305—Radar Target Recognition Technology Based on Deep Learning [基金-61404130305-基于深度学习的雷达目标识别技术]," *Whole Military Weapons and Equipment Purchase Information Net* [全军武器装备采购信息网], April 11, 2017.

enable it to leverage deep learning and model generation to identify underwater targets using limited acoustic data.[28]

Finally, the PLA is interested in data visualization capabilities. We uncovered references in articles that emphasized the importance of data visualization and integration in command platforms. Although we do not have access to these articles, they were authored by the Equipment College Complicated Electronic System Simulation Laboratory, the PLAAF Command College, the Liberation Army University and Technology Communications Engineering Department, and the 28th Research Institute of the China Electronics Technology Group Corporation (under the direct control of MIIT).

Equipment and Maintenance

The PLA believes that national defense big data will be helpful in both the procurement and maintenance of military equipment. According to military scholars, the PLA should strengthen its military equipment with big data analysis.[29] They suggest that, even though wars are fought with hardware, software will be the critical factor in whether these systems are ultimately effective.

Regarding equipment procurement, the PLA has commissioned work to create a supply-chain simulation and management system optimized using big data feedback and analysis, as well as software that uses big data to analyze and visualize business processes.[30] Sepa-

---

[28] "Naval Innovation—30202021401—Underwater Sound Detection and Recognition Based on Big Data [海军创新-30202021401-基于大数据的水声探测与识别技术]," *Whole Military Weapons and Equipment Purchase Information Net* [全军武器装备采购信息网], March 31, 2017. Also see "Fund—61404160301—Underwater Learning Target Recognition Method Based on Deep Learning and Generating Modeling (Key Points) [基金—61404160301—基于深度学习与生成式建模的水中目标识别方法（重点）]," *Whole Military Weapons and Equipment Purchase Information Net* [全军武器装备采购信息网], August 1, 2016.

[29] Liu Junjie [刘俊杰], Zhang Wenjun [张文军], and Chen Zhang [陈张], "Impact of Big Data on Military Equipment Construction and Development [大数据对军事装备建设与发展的影响]," *Journal of the Military Transportation University* [军事交通学院学报], Vol. 10, 2015.

[30] "Production Process Simulation and Control System Based on Big Data [基于大数据的生产过程仿真和控制系统]," *Whole Military Weapons and Equipment Purchase Information*

rately, a Chinese military scholar argued that the PLAN should build a smart manufacturing system for warships and warship components, including image analysis to identify hull failures and three-dimensional modeling precise enough to serve as a basis for assembly.[31] The modeling software should add needed systems autonomously. These features should improve both efficiency of production and equipment consistency by 30 percent. More broadly, according to another article, the PLA envisioned big data–enabled organization of China's defense industry.[32] This initiative would identify business departments' big data needs and create a model system that uses legal and technically feasible methods for these departments to obtain, store, analyze, and visualize those data. This system would help with equipment, logistics, mobilization, recruiting, training, technical innovation, and civil-military joint business work.

The PLA also has high hopes for big data support for equipment maintenance. For example, one project intends to collect data on up to 300 parameters, including system information, malfunctions, and maintenance records, to provide very early warnings of equipment failure with 70 percent accuracy.[33] Another project sought to employ big

---

Net [全军武器装备采购信息网], November 22, 2016; "Autonomous Business Data Analysis and Visualization Platform Software Purchasing Requirements [商业智能数据可视分析平台软件采购需求]," *Whole Military Weapons and Equipment Purchase Information Net* [全军武器装备采购信息网], April 10, 2019.

[31] "Naval Innovation—30205020708—Intelligent Control Technology for Construction Process Based on Big Data Analysis [海军创新–30205020708–基于大数据分析的建造过程智能管控技术]," *Whole Military Weapons and Equipment Purchase Information Net* [全军武器装备采购信息网], March 31, 2017.

[32] "Business-Oriented Big Data Mining Analysis [业务导向的大数据挖掘分析]," *Whole Military Weapons and Equipment Purchase Information Net* [全军武器装备采购信息网], April 21, 2017.

[33] "Common—41402050301—System-Level Product Fault Symptom Discovery and Fault Prediction Research Based on Big Data [共用–41402050301–基于大数据的系统级产品故障征兆发现与故障预测研究]," *Whole Military Weapons and Equipment Purchase Information Net* [全军武器装备采购信息网], May 23, 2017.

data, AI, and image recognition to identify cracks in engine propeller and impeller blades with 90 percent accuracy.[34]

Military Health Care and Mobilization

In the area of military health care, the PLA General Hospital and Peking University coestablished China's first National Laboratory of Medical Big Data Applied Technology. This occurred under the guidance of the NDRC's High-Tech Industry Department and the Central Military Commission's Logistics Support Department's Health Bureau.[35] Separately, the Special Warfare College Scientific Research Department planned to use big data to assess the likelihood of military sports training injuries and to improve risk management.[36]

At least two projects pertain to how big data might enhance China's mobilization efforts. The Fujian Electrical Engineering Group explored how the internet and automated data collection could improve China's understanding of its mobilization potential.[37] Another article discussed the National Civil Air Defense Office and its plans to complete infrastructure construction of a national big data platform for civil air defense by 2019.[38] This would entail the formulation of data standards and the establishment of civil air defense data centers at the national, provincial, and municipal levels. As of July 2020, Chinese

---

[34] "303060302—Air Force Equipment Pre-Research Innovation—Research on Engine Blade Crack Detection Based on Automatic Image Recognition [303060302-空军装备预研创新-基于自动图像识别的发动机叶片裂纹检测研究]," *Whole Military Weapons and Equipment Purchase Information Net* [全军武器装备采购信息网], September 1, 2017.

[35] Wang Junping [王君平] and Luo Guojin [罗国金], "China's First Medical Big Data Applied Technology Laboratory Established at the PLA General Hospital [国内首家医疗大数据应用技术国家工程实验室在解放军总医院成立]," *People's Daily*, November 26, 2017.

[36] Wang Wang [王王], "Based on the Risk of Military Sports Training Under Big Data Management Research [基于大数据下的军事体育训练风险管理初探]," *Journal of Military Physical Education and Sports* [军事体育学报], Vol. 1, 2017.

[37] Zhong Jun [钟军], "Exploring the Use of Big Data to Innovate the Investigation of the Country's Mobilization Potential [关于利用大数据创新国防动员潜力调查工作模式的探索]," *Information Technology and Informationization* [信息技术与信息化], Vol. 9, 2016.

[38] An Chunhong [安春红], "Civil Air Defense Big Data Platform Will Be Completed Before 2019 [人民防空大数据平台2019年前初步建成]," *China National Defense News* [中国国防报], January 10, 2017.

provinces seem to be continuing to improve their civil air defense big data systems.[39]

Training and Recruitment

The PLA clearly sees implications of big data analysis for achieving training and recruitment goals. According to an article from the 96754 Military Political Work Unit, big data can be used in political work and education to track soldiers' actions and thoughts, individualize education, and better evaluate education.[40] In another case, a training base in the Guangzhou Military Region used a database containing various details on such matters as family backgrounds, hobbies and interests, social media postings, and day-to-day thoughts and behavior to optimize political coursework.[41] Notably, the Central Police Academy released an article pointing out similar applications of big data in education for monitoring the daily activities, thoughts and political education, and mental and physical health of students.[42]

In the future, actual training events also might be managed and supported, to some extent, by big data analysis. While conducting an air and missile-defense training exercise, for instance, a detachment of the South Seas fleet used ship–air, ship–ship, and ship–shore data links to develop an integrated "data battlefield." The detachment used data collected previously by data-collection teams and used ship, equipment, and personnel performance data to digitize the battlefield

[39] Jiangsu Province Civil Air Defense General Office, Command and Information Office [省人防办综合处、指挥和信息化处], "Provincial Civil Air Defense Office Convenes Conference on 'Research Into Civil Air Defense Command Information Systems Based on Big Data [省人防办召开《基于大数据支撑的人防指挥信息系统研究》开题评审会]," Jiangsu Provincial Civil Defense Bureau, webpage, July 24, 2020.

[40] Ding Jiayou [丁佳友], "Using Big Data in Ideological and Political Education [大数据在思想政治教育中的运用]," Political Work Studies [政工学刊], Vol. 8, 2017.

[41] He Weili [何伟理], "Building 'Big Data' for 'Living Thoughts' [给 "或思想" 建立大数据]," Warrior News [战士报], August 31, 2015.

[42] Chai Ruobing [柴若冰] and Ma Guofu [马国富], "Using the Central Police Academy as an Example to Explore the Use of Big Data to Manage a Police Academy [大数据在警察院校警务化管理中的应用探析以中央司法警官学院为例]," Statistics and Management [统计与管理], Vol. 5, 2016.

environment and provide an accurate basis for after-action review processes.[43] Additionally, PLAAF units of the Central Theater Command organized 129 sorties operating from air bases as far as several thousand kilometers away from vehicle-borne command modules during the PLA's August 2017 parade at Zhurihe Training Base. The command modules conducted large amounts of data processing to determine the most-optimal flight routes to ensure precise and detailed command operations.[44]

The PLA further hopes to enhance officer professionalization using big data. In one example, the Shijiazhuang Mechanized Infantry School and the Hebei Media University sought to use big data to improve long-distance education, teaching methods, and educational resource allocation.[45] An article from the PLAAF Early Warning College assessed how the U.S. military was leveraging big data in professional training and how the PLA could follow suit.[46] The Nanjing Politics College Shanghai Campus also released a paper on big data in military human resource decisionmaking.[47]

Regarding PLA recruitment, a military department based in Hailin, Heilongjiang, for instance, used a big data platform to identify highly educated young persons of appropriate age. This improved

---

[43] Li Youtao [黎友陶], "'Data Wars' Play Out in Distant Ocean ['数据战场' 亮剑远海大洋]," *People's Liberation Army Daily*, May 19, 2016.

[44] "'Big Data' Transmits the Air Force's Strategic Transition ['大数据' 透射空军战略转型]," *Science and Technology Daily*, July 31, 2017.

[45] Wang Pingli [王萍丽], Wu Zheng [吴政], and Wu Yinghao [吴英昊], "Researching Problems of Modern Military Distance Education in an Era of Big Data [大数据时代军队现代远程教育发展问题研究]," *Continuing Education* [继续教育], Vol. 12, 2014.

[46] Tan Shaoying [谈少盈], Li Xiaoping [李小平], and Wang Pinpin [王品品], "Practice of the U.S. Military's Using Big Data for Promoting Military Vocational Education and Their Enlightenments [美军运用大数据促进军事职业教育的做法及启示]," *Journal of the Air Force Early Warning Academy* [空军预警学院学报], Vol. 4, 2016.

[47] Xing Jinrong [邢金融] and Zhang Yiming [张一明], "Using Big Data to Improve the Effectiveness of Military HR [运用大数据提升军事人力资源管理效能]," *Theoretical Studies on PLA Political Work* [军队政工理论研究], Vol. 5, 2016.

the PLA's ability to send recruitment materials on a targeted basis over social media at predetermined intervals.[48]

Modeling and Simulation

Modeling and simulation make up another area of interest for the PLA in national defense big data. For example, according to an ambitious article from the National Defense Technology University Information Systems and Management School, the PLA should create a "cyber-physical social system" for military affairs.[49] In such a system, a virtual version of the battlespace would be created and constantly refined for accuracy. This would help train commanders and test strategies or tactics. It could also be tied to units in the actual battlefield to track their movements and better control them. Such a system could enable a commander to fire missiles with the push of a button and would be as essential in military affairs as smart control processes are in manufacturing. Moreover, at the 24th meeting of the China (Military) Systems Engineering Professional Association, participants discussed big data in the context of combat evaluation and combat experiments, suggesting a possible link between these concepts.[50] Last, we found that the PLA proposed a project in 2017 to research methods and the general state of the field in using AI and deep learning in equipment modeling and simulation.[51]

---

[48] Liu Jianwei [刘建伟], "In the Era of Big Data, How Can the Work of Armed Forces Departments Be Precisely Upgraded? [大数据时代, 武装工作如何精准发力]," *People's Liberation Army Daily*, April 27, 2017.

[49] Wang Feiyue [王飞跃], "The Coming Revolution in National Defense Weaponry and Systems: From 3-D Printing to Parallel Military Systems [国防装备与系统的未来变革: 从3D打印到平行军事体系]," *National Defense Science and Technology* [国防科技], Vol. 3, 2013.

[50] Liu Xujiang [刘书江], Zhao Cunru [赵存如], and Li Ning [李宁], "Summary of the 24th Annual Meeting of the China Systems Engineering Academy Military Systems Engineering Professional Group [中国系统工程学会军事系统工程专业委员会第二十四届学术年会成果综述]," *Military Operations Systems Engineering* [军事运筹与系统工程], Vol. 4, 2014.

[51] "Key Laboratory Fund—61420080104—Application of Artificial Intelligence Based on Deep Learning in Simulation of Army Equipment System [重点实验室基金-61420080104-基于深度学习的人工智能技术在陆军装备体系仿真中的应用研究]," *Whole Military Weapons and Equipment Purchase Information Net* [全军武器装备采购信息网], May 19, 2017.

Cybersecurity

Cybersecurity appears to be another major area of focus the PLA's push on big data. For example, we discovered a PLAAF project seeking to collect behavioral and safety data from all end-point terminals in real time to identify threats.[52] This system should be able to do threat modeling using online information and then go upstream to find the source of a problem. In another case, the PLA sought to develop cyber defense and multidomain security technologies.[53] A 2019 PLA research project aims to use adversarial machine learning processes to build algorithms capable of identifying malicious data introduced into automated systems, as well as other algorithms that might malfunction for the PLA under operational conditions.[54] To improve hardware security, the PLA has commissioned the creation of software that can identify when circuits or chips have been tampered with by analyzing pictures of them.[55]

More broadly, the PLA clearly prioritizes cyber warfare and the integration of data obtained from these efforts with other data from related or different warfighting domains. The most notable example of this is the PLA's establishment in December 2015 of the PLA Strategic Support Force (PLASSF). The PLASSF is responsible for integrat-

---

[52] "303060501—Air Force Equipment and Research Innovation—Air Force Information Network End-Point Security Response and Monitoring Big Data System [303060501-空军装备预研创新-空军信息网络终端安全大数据分析响应与监控系统]," *Whole Military Weapons and Equipment Purchase Information Net* [全军武器装备采购信息网], August 10, 2017.

[53] "315075703 Automated System Data and Algorithm Safety Evaluation Technology [315075703智能系统数据与算法安全检测技术]," *Whole Military Weapons and Equipment Purchase Information Net* [全军武器装备采购信息网], February 14, 2019.

[54] "Key Laboratory Fund—61421030206—Research on Big Data Security and Privacy Protection Technology [重点实验室基金-61421030206-大数据安全及隐私保护技术研究]," *Whole Military Weapons and Equipment Purchase Information Net* [全军武器装备采购信息网], May 19, 2017.

[55] "31512050403 Machine Learning Technology to Detect Trojan Horses in Integrated Circuits [31512050403基于机器学习的集成电路硬件木马版图检测技术]," *Whole Military Weapons and Equipment Purchase Information Net* [全军武器装备采购信息网], April 30, 2019.

ing cyber data with EM and space warfare information.[56] This is a uniquely Chinese arrangement with an ambiguous chance of success. Regardless, the creation of such an organization underscores just how seriously—and how boldly—Beijing is thinking about national big data integration in support of joint military operations.

Next Up: Transitioning from Informatization to Intelligentization

In the coming years, China hopes to have mastered national defense big data sufficiently to control or even dominate the informationized warfare environment against great powers. This, however, is merely the beginning. National defense big data also undergirds Beijing's longer-term effort, articulated by President Xi in his 19th Party Congress speech, to ultimately become the global center for AI by 2030. Doing so includes creating an intelligentized military.[57]

In truth, Beijing still has a long way to go to achieve the great potential it sees in automated decision aids and decisionmaking. Nevertheless, in many areas, Beijing is actively considering the implications of AI technology for military applications.[58] The PLA wants to create a digital staff officer who is integrated into its Joint Operations Command System to perform rapid information integration and

---

[56] For more on the PLASSF, see Kevin L. Pollpeter, Michael S. Chase, and Eric Heginbotham, *The Creation of the PLA Strategic Support Force and Its Implications for Chinese Military Space Operations*, Santa Monica, Calif.: RAND Corporation, RR-2058-AF, 2017.

[57] See, for example, China Military Science Editorial Department [中国军事科学 编辑部], "A Summary of the Workshop on the Game Between AlphaGo and Lee Sedol and the Intelligentization of Military Command and Decision-Making [围棋人机大战与军事指挥决策智能化研讨会观点综述]," *China Military Science* [中国军事科学], April 2, 2016.

[58] For an authoritative listing and analysis of China's nascent military AI capabilities, see Elsa B. Kania, *Battlefield Singularity: Artificial Intelligence, Military Revolution, and China's Future Military Power*, Washington, D.C.: Center for a New American Security, November 28, 2017. For a broader look at China's AI plans across all fields, including the military, see Jeffrey Ding, *Deciphering China's AI Dream: The Context, Components, and Consequences of China's Strategy to Lead the World in AI*, Oxford, UK: Future of Humanity Institute, University of Oxford, March 2018.

planning.[59] The hope is that, one day, this digital staff officer will be capable of offering command recommendations to increase speed and accuracy of decisions, along the lines of Defense Advanced Research Projects Agency's Deep Green program. Recent PLA research projects have begun taking steps to build algorithms that can help commanders use data to make better battlefield decisions. Two such projects aim to use machine learning algorithms to extract optimal tactics or strategies from the data generated by past operations.[60] Another project sought to achieve a similar result using dueling algorithms, which would hone their skills by playing iterative, realistic tactical simulation games against one another.[61] The PLA is also looking into improving wargaming with AI-enabled smart adversaries and realistic training.[62] To enable these capabilities, the PLA is seeking to develop smaller, lighter, and faster hardware so that its computers can conduct complex calculations in operational settings fast enough to enable Chinese commanders to observe, orient, decide, and act (OODA) more rapidly than their opponents.[63] It is further examining plans to enhance natural language processing, automated translation, and analysis of social

---

[59] Kania, 2017.

[60] "Space Flight System Modeling Major Laboratory Fund—6142002302—Autonomous Systems to Identify Optimal Paths to Victory Based on Shifting Situations [航天系统仿真重点实验室基金-6142002302-基于事件演化的智能化制胜规则寻优方法]," *Whole Military Weapons and Equipment Purchase Information Net* [全军武器装备采购信息网], November 25, 2018; "31511120201 Autonomous Technology to Generate, Optimize, and Evaluate Military Knowledge Based on Machine Learning [31511120201基于机器学习的军事知识生成、演化与评估技术]," *Whole Military Weapons and Equipment Purchase Information Net* [全军武器装备采购信息网], April 30, 2019.

[61] "31505550302 Learning from and Modeling Autonomous Adversarial Games [31505550302面向智能博弈的对抗策略建模与学习技术]," *Whole Military Weapons and Equipment Purchase Information Net* [全军武器装备采购信息网], February 14, 2019.

[62] Hu Xiaofeng, He Xiaoyuan, and Tao Jiuyang, "Alpha Gou's Breakthrough and the Deductive Challenge of War Games [AlphaGo的突破与兵棋推演的挑战]," *Science and Technology Review* [科技导报] , Vol. 35, No. 17, 2017, p. 58.

[63] "31511020105 Embedded Platforms for Smart Computing [31511020105装备嵌入式智能计算平台技术]," *Whole Military Weapons and Equipment Purchase Information Net* [全军武器装备采购信息网], December 23, 2017. Note that the description of this project explicitly references the OODA loop.

media platforms.[64] Beijing is also exploring *cognitive radio,* the use of AI to protect against jamming and to better jam enemy frequencies.[65]

Beijing believes that AI holds important implications for military hardware as well. It is looking into smarter AI cruise missiles; highly autonomous unmanned aerial vehicles; swarming unmanned aerial vehicles; highly autonomous off-road armed and unarmed unmanned ground vehicles; anti-artillery or missile laser systems capable of autonomously identifying, tracking, and engaging low-altitude targets; and highly autonomous long-range surface and underwater unmanned vehicles.[66] Finally, Beijing is considering operating systems and chips for AI systems, autonomous system safety, manned–unmanned teaming command and control, and autonomously coordinated operations with many types of drones.[67] Successful management and employment of national defense big data are the first in a likely series of challenging steps toward development of all these, and other, AI systems.

---

[64] "Artificial Intelligence Project 2—Analysis of Critical Patents in Natural Language Processing [人工智能系列2——自然语言处理关键技术专利分析]," *Whole Military Weapons and Equipment Purchase Information Net* [全军武器装备采购信息网], December 23, 2017.

[65] Kania, 2017.

[66] Kania, 2017. Also see Abhijit Singh, "Is China Really Building Missiles with Artificial Intelligence?" *The Diplomat,* September 21, 2016; "Army Advanced Research—0243—Independent Coordination for Multiple Drones [陆军预研-0243-无人机多机自主协同技术]," *Whole Military Weapons and Equipment Purchase Information Net* [全军武器装备采购信息网], July 27, 2016; Jeffrey Lin and P. W. Singer, "China's New Military Robots Pack More Robots Inside (Starcraft-Style)," *Popular Science,* November 11, 2014; Jeffrey Lin and P. W. Singer, "New Chinese Laser Weapon Stars on TV," *Popular Science,* November 25, 2015; "Major Laboratory Fund—61422150101—AI Navigation Methods for Unmanned Maritime Navigation [重点实验室基金-61422150101-面向水中无人航行器的人工智能方法]," *Whole Military Weapons and Equipment Purchase Information Net* [全军武器装备采购信息网], May 19, 2017; "An Age in Which We Reach a Depth of 1,000 Meters," *IQIVI,* November 19, 2016.

[67] State Council, "Plan for Developing a New Generation of AI [新一代人工智能发展规划]," July 8, 2017; "Major Laboratory Fund—61423011001—Distribution and Resource Optimization and Path Planning for Multiple Drone Cooperative Missions [重点实验室基金-61423011001-异构多无人机协同任务分配、资源优化和路径规划系统]," *Whole Military Weapons and Equipment Purchase Information Net* [全军武器装备采购信息网], May 19, 2017.

CHAPTER FIVE

Concluding Thoughts and Future Research

Beijing clearly has high hopes for big data analytics. The common vision among Chinese leaders is that employment of big data will play an instrumental role in helping China become a true great power. They further believe, however, that becoming a global leader in the informationized era can take China only so far. Beijing seeks to build on big data analytic technologies and skills to become, by 2030, the global center for AI or, as Chinese leaders call it, *intelligentized decisionmaking*.

In the meantime, and judging from our two case studies, we believe that Beijing has a deep understanding of the value of integrating big data into government and military activities. Whether in the areas of crime prevention and controlling the behavior of its citizens or in improving the PLA's ability to conduct joint military operations, there is an impressive variety of big data analytic programs that have either been proposed or are being implemented in China. Furthermore, as this report demonstrates, openly available Chinese primary sources are extensive and, at times, fairly detailed on the specific plans for big data initiatives. We did encounter several situations in which either details were removed from their original web sources or the information requested was denied for sensitivity reasons. In the future, we would look to supplement our unclassified findings with clandestinely acquired information to obtain a more fulsome picture of Chinese big data efforts in these domains.

Drawing on our two case studies, we believe that further research into the following questions would provide greater insight into Chinese involvement and investment in big data analytics:

- *How might China externally wield its evolving big data capabilities to monitor and control its population?* Using big data, what might Beijing be able to learn about potential adversaries to coerce or otherwise influence domestic events in these countries? For many decades, Beijing has been employing "united front" tactics against the Taiwanese people to divide them in an attempt to make them more amenable to Chinese demands on the sovereignty issue.[1] The extent to which China's new big data analysis capabilities might further enhance united front activities, both in peace and in wartime, is unclear. Similarly, in April 2015, Chinese intelligence services successfully hacked the U.S. Office of Personnel Management (OPM), providing Beijing with enormous data sets on U.S. personnel that could also prove useful.[2] Given recent revelations from the intelligence community that Russia used social media to attempt to influence the outcome of the U.S. presidential election, it is possible that Beijing would similarly use this personal data to launch targeted propaganda and disinformation campaigns during future elections. It is equally possible that Beijing might leverage hacked OPM data in support of military operations in a future armed conflict with the United States.

- *How does China's evolving big data analytic capability rank in comparison with that of the United States in the military domain?* A detailed net assessment of the PLA versus the U.S. military's ability to exploit national defense big data would assess existing infrastructure and technologies and the level of training and expertise of personnel in both countries to leverage big data in warfighting. This analysis would also consider and compare future invest-

---

[1] See, for example, Lauren Dickey, "Can Taiwan Defend Identity from China's United Front Tactics?" *News Lens*, blog post, April 4, 2018.

[2] Although China is not specifically mentioned as the perpetrator of the attack, an official account of OPM vulnerabilities enabling the attack can be found in Committee on Oversight and Government Reform, U.S. House of Representatives, *The OPM Data Breach: How the Government Jeopardized Our National Security for More Than a Generation*, Washington, D.C., majority staff report, September 7, 2016. For an analysis of China's role in the hack, see, for example, Brendan I. Koener, "Inside the Cyberattack That Shocked the U.S. Government," *Wired*, October 23, 2016.

ments in big data analytics to determine future trend lines and likely scenarios out to 2030.

Beyond these possible follow-on studies for our two case studies, there are at least three other, separate areas of potential interest on big data analytics:

- *How is China leveraging big data analysis in support of its R&D processes?* The decisionmaking behind Beijing's R&D processes is notoriously opaque. A better understanding of the big data analytic capabilities that are integrated into China's R&D process might shed light on factors influencing and shaping investment decisions. It might also enable the United States to better identify the types of PLA systems in R&D.
- *How does China assess technological or economic trends using big data analytics?* China's drive to build indigenous innovative technologies and attract global business through its cornerstone Belt and Road Initiative would almost certainly benefit from big data analysis. An assessment of how big data analytics is used in economic and R&D decisionmaking could give the United States a greater appreciation for the reasoning behind these policies and enable Washington to either complement or compete with them.
- *How does Chinese leadership think about big data–enabled government services and their implications for domestic stability?* A common theme throughout the publicly available Chinese literature on big data analysis is the need to leverage this capability to enhance the government's online services. Known as eGoverment services, the concept also has implications for reducing the chance for social unrest that might threaten the regime and domestic stability.

References

"2017 'Fang Huiju' Visit Newsletter Issue 5 20160301 [2017师市 "访惠聚" 简报 05期-20160301]," March 1, 2016.

"303060302—Air Force Equipment Pre-Research Innovation—Research on Engine Blade Crack Detection Based on Automatic Image Recognition [303060302-空军装备预研创新-基于自动图像识别的发动机叶片裂纹检测研究]," *Whole Military Weapons and Equipment Purchase Information Net* [全军武器装备采购信息网], September 1, 2017.

"303060501—Air Force Equipment and Research Innovation—Air Force Information Network End-Point Security Response and Monitoring Big Data System [303060501-空军装备预研创新-空军信息网络终端安全大数据分析响应与监控系统]," *Whole Military Weapons and Equipment Purchase Information Net* [全军武器装备采购信息网], August 10, 2017.

"31505550302 Learning from and Modeling Autonomous Adversarial Games [31505550302面向智能博弈的对抗策略建模与学习技术]," *Whole Military Weapons and Equipment Purchase Information Net* [全军武器装备采购信息网], February 14, 2019.

"315075703 Automated System Data and Algorithm Safety Evaluation Technology [315075703智能系统数据与算法安全检测技术]," *Whole Military Weapons and Equipment Purchase Information Net* [全军武器装备采购信息网], February 14, 2019.

"31511020105 Embedded Platforms for Smart Computing [31511020105装备嵌入式智能计算平台技术]," *Whole Military Weapons and Equipment Purchase Information Net* [全军武器装备采购信息网], December 23, 2017.

"31511120201 Autonomous Technology to Generate, Optimize, and Evaluate Military Knowledge Based on Machine Learning [31511120201基于机器学习的军事知识生成、演化与评估技术]," *Whole Military Weapons and Equipment Purchase Information Net* [全军武器装备采购信息网], April 30, 2019.

"31512050403 Machine Learning Technology to Detect Trojan Horses in Integrated Circuits [31512050403基于机器学习的集成电路硬件木马版图检测技术]," *Whole Military Weapons and Equipment Purchase Information Net* [全军武器装备采购信息网], April 30, 2019.

Alibaba Group, "Ant Financial Unveils China's First Credit-Scoring System Using Online Data," press release, Hangzhou, China, January 28, 2015. As of May 1, 2020:
https://www.alibabagroup.com/en/news/article?news=p150128

"An Age in Which We Reach a Depth of 1,000 Meters," *IQIVI*, November 19, 2016. As of October 14, 2018:
https://www.iqiyi.com/v_19rrly3kcc.html

"An Anti-Terrorism Risk Analysis Method Based on Bayesian Theory [一种基于贝叶斯理论的反恐风险分析方法]," *China National Knowledge Infrastructure*, September 2017. As of May 8, 2018:
http://www.cnki.com.cn/Article/CJFDTotal-QBZZ201709003.htm

An Chunhong [安春红], "Civil Air Defense Big Data Platform Will Be Completed Before 2019 [人民防空大数据平台2019年前初步建成]," *China National Defense News* [中国国防报], January 10, 2017. As of May 15, 2018:
http://www.81.cn/jmywyl/2017-01/10/content_7444744.htm

"Army Advanced Research—0243—Independent Coordination for Multiple Drones [陆军预研-0243-无人机多机自主协同技术]," *Whole Military Weapons and Equipment Purchase Information Net* [全军武器装备采购信息网], July 27, 2016.

"Artificial Intelligence Project 2—Analysis of Critical Patents in Natural Language Processing [人工智能系列2——自然语言处理关键技术专利分析]," *Whole Military Weapons and Equipment Purchase Information Net* [全军武器装备采购信息网], December 23, 2017.

"Artificial Intelligence Series 3—Patent Analysis of Key Technologies in Computer Vision [人工智能系列3—计算机视觉关键技术专利分析]," *Whole Military Weapons and Equipment Purchase Information Net* [全军武器装备采购信息网], December 23, 2017.

"Autonomous Business Data Analysis and Visualization Platform Software Purchasing Requirements [商业智能数据可视分析平台软件采购需求]," *Whole Military Weapons and Equipment Purchase Information Net* [全军武器装备采购信息网], April 10, 2019.

"Big Data Machine [大数据一体机]," *Whole Military Weapons and Equipment Purchase Information Net* [全军武器装备采购信息网], April 5, 2016.

"'Big Data' Transmits the Air Force's Strategic Transition ['大数据'透射空军战略转型]," *Science and Technology Daily*, July 31, 2017. As of February 18, 2018:
http://scitech.people.com.cn/n1/2017/0731/c1057-29438732.html

Botsman, Rachel, "Big Data Meets Big Brother as China Moves to Rate Its Citizens," *Wired UK*, October 21, 2017.

"Business-Oriented Big Data Mining Analysis [业务导向的大数据挖掘分析]," *Whole Military Weapons and Equipment Purchase Information Net* [全军武器装备采购信息网], April 21, 2017.

Central People's Government [中华人民共和国中央人民政府], "Our Nation Will Build a 'Unified Picture' Government Affairs Geographic Information Big Data System [我国将建设政务地理信息大数据 "一张图"]," December 26, 2017.

Chai Ruobing [柴若冰] and Ma Guofu [马国富], "Using the Central Police Academy as an Example to Explore the Use of Big Data to Manage a Police Academy [大数据在警察院校警务化管理中的应用探析以中央司法警官学院为例]," *Statistics and Management* [统计与管理], Vol. 5, 2016.

Cheng Rong [程荣] and Pei Xian [裴贤], "National Defense Big Data: The Intelligent Core That Protects National Security [国防大数据：守护国家安全的智慧芯]," *People's Liberation Army Daily* [解放军日报], January 11, 2017. As of May 10, 2018:
http://www.81.cn/jmywyl/2017-01/11/content_7446932.htm

Chin, Josh, and Liza Lin, "China's All-Seeing Surveillance State Is Reading Its Citizens' Faces," *Straits Times*, July 8, 2017.

"China Invents the Digital Totalitarian State," *The Economist*, December 17, 2016.

"China: Big Data Fuels Crackdown in Minority Region," Human Rights Watch, blog post, February 26, 2018. As of May 7, 2018:
https://www.hrw.org/news/2018/02/26/
china-big-data-fuels-crackdown-minority-region

"China Maps Out AI Development Plan," Xinhua, July 20, 2017.

"China: Minority Region Collects DNA from Millions: Private Information Gathered by Police, Under Guise of Public Health Program," Human Rights Watch, blog post, December 13, 2017. As of October 3, 2018:
https://www.hrw.org/news/2017/12/13/china-minority-region-collects-dna-millions

"China: Police 'Big Data' Systems Violate Privacy, Target Dissent," Human Rights Watch, blog post, November 19, 2017. As of October 11, 2018:
https://www.hrw.org/news/2017/11/19/
china-police-big-data-systems-violate-privacy-target-dissent

"China: Xi Jinping Chairs Second Collective Study Session of Politburo on National Big Data Strategy," Xinhua, CHR2017120927141422, December 9, 2017.

China Military Science Editorial Department [中国军事科学 编辑部], "A Summary of the Workshop on the Game Between AlphaGo and Lee Sedol and the Intelligentization of Military Command and Decision-Making [围棋人机大战与军事指挥决策智能化研讨会观点综述]," *China Military Science*, April 2, 2016.

"China Must Accelerate Implementation of Big Data Strategy: Xi," Xinhua, December 9, 2017.

"China's Algorithms of Repression: Reverse-Engineering a Xinjiang Police Mass Surveillance App," Human Rights Watch, May 1, 2019. As of September 11, 2019: https://www.hrw.org/report/2019/05/02/chinas-algorithms-repression/reverse-engineering-xinjiang-police-mass

Committee on Oversight and Government Reform, U.S. House of Representatives, *The OPM Data Breach: How the Government Jeopardized Our National Security for More Than a Generation*, Washington, D.C., majority staff report, September 7, 2016.

"Common—41402050301—System-Level Product Fault Symptom Discovery and Fault Prediction Research Based on Big Data [共用-41402050301-基于大数据的系统级产品故障征兆发现与故障预测研究]," *Whole Military Weapons and Equipment Purchase Information Net* [全军武器装备采购信息网], May 23, 2017.

Dickey, Lauren, "Can Taiwan Defend Identity from China's United Front Tactics?" *News Lens*, blog post, April 4, 2018. As of October 11, 2018: https://international.thenewslens.com/article/92905

Ding, Jeffrey, *Deciphering China's AI Dream: The Context, Components, and Consequences of China's Strategy to Lead the World in AI*, Oxford, UK: Future of Humanity Institute, University of Oxford, March 2018.

Ding Jiayou [丁佳友], "Using Big Data in Ideological and Political Education [大数据在思想政治教育中的运用]," *Political Work Studies* [政工学刊] , Vol. 8, 2017.

"Ebin County, Minta County, 'Integrated Joint Combat Platform' Video Surveillance Construction Project Publicity Results [塔城区额敏县"一体化联合作战平台"视频监控建设项目成交结果公示]," webpage, March 21, 2017. As of May 8, 2018: http://bidding.its114.com/zhongbiao/Safecity1/2017_03_85923.html

Engstrom, Jeffrey, *Systems Confrontation and System Destruction Warfare: How the Chinese People's Liberation Army Seeks to Wage Modern Warfare*, Santa Monica, Calif.: RAND Corporation, RR-1708-OSD, 2018. As of October 11, 2018: https://www.rand.org/pubs/research_reports/RR1708.html

"Facial Recognition Identifies Unlicensed Drivers in Shanghai," Xinhua, December 6, 2017.

Falkvinge, Rick, "In China, Your Credit Score Is Now Affected by Your Political Opinions—and Your Friends' Political Opinions," *Privacy News Online*, blog post, October 3, 2015. As of October 11, 2018: https://www.privateinternetaccess.com/blog/2015/10/in-china-your-credit-score-is-now-affected-by-your-political-opinions-and-your-friends-political-opinions/

Fravel, M. Taylor, "China's New Military Strategy: 'Winning Informationized Local Wars,'" *China Brief*, Vol. 15, No. 13, July 2, 2015. As of October 11, 2018: https://jamestown.org/program/chinas-new-military-strategy-winning-informationized-local-wars/

"From Ale to Jail: Facial Recognition Catches Criminals at China Beer Festival," *The Guardian*, September 1, 2017. As of October 11, 2018: https://www.theguardian.com/world/2017/sep/01/facial-recognition-china-beer-festival

Fu Zhong-li [傅中力], Zhuang Huang [张煌], and Li Po [李坡], "National Security and Military Strategy Selection in an Era of Big Data [大数据时代的国家安全与军事战略选择]," *National Defense Science and Technology*, Vol. 2, 2013.

"Full Text of Xi Jinping's Report at the 19th CPC National Congress," Xinhua, November 3, 2017.

"Fund—61401370502—Research on Signal Feature Extraction Based on Deep Learning [基金-61401370502-基于深度学习的信号特征提取技术研究]," *Whole Military Weapons and Equipment Purchase Information Net* [全军武器装备采购信息网], August 1, 2016.

"Fund—61404130305—Radar Target Recognition Technology Based on Deep Learning [基金-61404130305-基于深度学习的雷达目标识别技术]," *Whole Military Weapons and Equipment Purchase Information Net* [全军武器装备采购信息网], April 11, 2017.

"Fund—61404160301—Underwater Learning Target Recognition Method Based on Deep Learning and Generating Modeling (Key Points) [基金—61404160301—基于深度学习与生成式建模的水中目标识别方法（重点）]," *Whole Military Weapons and Equipment Purchase Information Net* [全军武器装备采购信息网], August 1, 2016.

Gao Lu [高路], "Credit Blacklists: Not the Solution to Every Social Problem [信用黑名单，不能啥都往里装]," *Qianjiang Evening News* [钱江晚报], trans. Ryan Soh and Jeffrey Ding for *ChinAI*, No. 61, July 30, 2019. As of April 22, 2020: https://chinai.substack.com/archive

Guo Jiguang [郭继光] and Huang Sheng [黄胜], "Study on Architecture of Big Data Based on Military Intelligence Analysis and Service System [基于大数据的军事情报分析与服务系统架构研究]," *Journal of the Chinese Academy of Electronics and Information Technology* [中国电子科学研究院学报], Vol. 4, 2017.

Han Ming [韩明], Yang Jibao [杨继宝], and Lu Xiang [卢祥], "The Era of Big Data War [大数据战时代]," *China New Telecommunications* [中国心通信], Vol. 11, 2017.

Hawkins, Amy, "Chinese Citizens Want Their Government to Rank Them," *Foreign Policy*, May 24, 2017. As of October 11, 2018: https://foreignpolicy.com/2017/05/24/chinese-citizens-want-the-government-to-rank-them/

He Weili [何伟理], "Building 'Big Data' for 'Living Thoughts' [给"或思想"建立大数据]," *Warrior News* [战士报], August 31, 2015.

He You [何友], Zhu Yangyong [朱扬勇], Zhao Peng [赵鹏], Chai Yong [柴勇], Liao Zhicheng [廖志成], Zhou Wei [周伟], Zhou Xiangdong [周向东], Wang Haipeng [王海鹏], Wang Wei [汪卫], Xiong Yun [熊赟], Xu Zhoujun [许舟军], Peng Xuan [彭煊], Meng Hui [孟晖], and Wang Shengjin [王生进], "Panorama of National Defense Big Data [国防大数据概论]," *Systems Engineering and Electronics* [系统工程与电子技术], Vol. 6, 2016.

Hetian Town Government, "Hetian Area Emergency Management Work Information Phase 1 [和田地区应急管理工作信息 第1期]," January 6, 2017.

"Hetian Public Security Bureau Public Security Checkpoint Project Single Source Procurement Pre-Winning Public Notice [和田市公安局治安检查站项目单一来源采购预中标公示公告]," February 6, 2017.

Hu Xiaofeng, He Xiaoyuan, and Tao Jiuyang, "Alpha Go's Breakthrough and the Deductive Challenge of War Games [AlphaGo的突破与兵棋推演的挑战]," *Science and Technology Review* [科技导报] , Vol. 35, No. 17, 2017, p. 58.

Hu Yong, "The Public Interest and Personal Privacy in a Time of Crisis (Part I)," Weixin, trans. Jeff Ding for *ChinAI*, No. 85, March 6, 2020a.

———, "The Public Interest and Personal Privacy in a Time of Crisis (Part II)," Weixin, trans. Jeff Ding for *ChinAI*, March 6, 2020b.

Hvistendahl, Mara, "Inside China's Vast New Experiment in Social Ranking," *Wired*, December 14, 2017. As of October 1, 2018:
https://www.wired.com/story/age-of-social-credit/

IBM, "Big Data Analytics," webpage, undated. As of October 11, 2018:
https://www.ibm.com/analytics/hadoop/big-data-analytics

"Identify 75 Religious Extreme Activities [识别75种宗教极端活动]," *Nanchang Gonganju* [南昌公安局], September 8, 2015.

Jakhar, Pratik, "Coronavirus: China's Tech Fights Back," *BBC Monitoring*, March 3, 2020. As of March 26, 2020:
https://www.bbc.com/news/technology-51717164

Jia Chong [贾冲], "Databases, Assisting High-Quality and Rapid Support [数据库, 助保障优质快速]," *Air Force Daily*, May 27, 2016.

Jiangsu Province Civil Air Defense General Office, Command and Information Office [省人防办综合处、指挥和信息化处], "Provincial Civil Air Defense Office Convenes Conference on 'Research Into Civil Air Defense Command Information Systems Based on Big Data [省人防办召开《基于大数据支撑的人防指挥信息系统研究》开题评审会]," Jiangsu Provincial Civil Defense Bureau, webpage, July 24, 2020.

Jiang Surong [蒋苏蓉], and Meng Jiangqiao [蓝江桥], "Timeout Prediction of the Schedule Method for Big Data of the Intelligence Analysis Based on Hadoop [Hadoop框架下的情报分析大数据调度超时预测方法]," *Computer Science* [计算机科学], Supp. 1, 2014.

Kania, Elsa B., *Battlefield Singularity: Artificial Intelligence, Military Revolution, and China's Future Military Power*, Washington, D.C.: Center for a New American Security, November 28, 2017.

"Key Laboratory Fund—61420080104—Application of Artificial Intelligence Based on Deep Learning in Simulation of Army Equipment System [重点实验室基金-61420080104-基于深度学习的人工智能技术在陆军装备体系仿真中的应用研究]," *Whole Military Weapons and Equipment Purchase Information Net,* May 19, 2017.

"Key Laboratory Fund—61421030206—Research on Big Data Security and Privacy Protection Technology [重点实验室基金-61421030206-大数据安全及隐私保护技术研究]," *Whole Military Weapons and Equipment Purchase Information Net* [全军武器装备采购信息网], May 19, 2017.

"Key Laboratory Fund—61421070104—Optical Information Fusion Technology Based on Big Data [重点实验室基金-61421070104-基于大数据的光电信息融合技术]," *Whole Military Weapons and Equipment Purchase Information Net* [全军武器装备采购信息网], May 19, 2017.

"Key Laboratory Fund—61425030202—Microwave Imaging Automatic Recognition Technology [重点实验室基金-61425030202-微波成像自动识别技术]," *Whole Military Weapons and Equipment Purchase Information Net* [全军武器装备采购信息网], May 19, 2017.

"Key Laboratory Fund—6142A010103—New Model of Spectral Matching for Ground Objects Supported by Multisource Remote Sensing Big Data [重点实验室基金-6142A010103-多源遥感大数据支持下的地物光谱匹配新模型研究]," *Whole Military Weapons and Equipment Purchase Information Net,* May 19, 2017.

Koener, Brendan I., "Inside the Cyberattack That Shocked the U.S. Government," *Wired*, October 23, 2016. As of October 11, 2018:
https://www.wired.com/2016/10/inside-cyberattack-shocked-us-government/

Li Chongdong, "Study on the Construction of the Military Decision-Making System Based on Large Data Support [基于大数据支持的军事决策系统构建研究]," *Software Engineering* [软件工程], Vol. 3, 2016.

Li Qiaoming, "Big Data: Making War Commanding Decisions More Scientific [大数据：让战争指挥决策更科学]," *People's Liberation Army Daily*, February 28, 2017. As of May 10, 2018:
http://www.81.cn/jmywyl/2017-02/28/content_7505090.htm

Li Youtao, "'Data Wars' Play Out in Distant Ocean ['数据战场'亮剑远海大洋]," *People's Liberation Army Daily*, May 19, 2016.

Lin, Jeffrey, and P. W. Singer, "China's New Military Robots Pack More Robots Inside (Starcraft-Style)," *Popular Science*, November 11, 2014. As of October 11, 2018:
https://www.popsci.com/blog-network/eastern-arsenal/
chinas-new-military-robots-pack-more-robots-inside-starcraft-style

———, "New Chinese Laser Weapon Stars on TV," *Popular Science*, November 25, 2015. As of October 11, 2018:
https://www.popsci.com/new-chinese-laser-weapon-stars-on-tv

Liu Jianwei, "In the Era of Big Data, How Can the Work of Armed Forces Departments Be Precisely Upgraded? [大数据时代，武装工作如何精准发力]," *Liberation Army Daily*, April 27, 2017. As of February 20, 2018:
http://www.81.cn/jmywyl/2017-04/27/content_7579223.htm

Liu Junjie [刘俊杰], Zhang Wenjun [张文军], and Chen Zhang [陈张], "Impact of Big Data on Military Equipment Construction and Development [大数据对军事装备建设与发展的影响]," *Journal of the Military Transportation University* [军事交通学院学报], Vol. 10, 2015.

Liu Linshan, "What Is the Function of Big Data in the Construction of a Modern National Defense and the Military? [大数据在国防和军队现代化建设中有何作用？]," *Liberation Army Daily*, February 1, 2018. As of February 15, 2018:
http://www.81.cn/jmywyl/2018-02/01/content_7928180.htm

Liu Xujiang [刘书江], Zhao Cunru [赵存如], and Li Ning [李宁], "Summary of the 24th Annual Meeting of the China Systems Engineering Academy Military Systems Engineering Professional Group [中国系统工程学会军事系统工程专业委员会第二十四届学术年会成果综述]," *Military Operations Systems Engineering* [军事运筹与系统工程], Vol. 4, 2014.

"Major Laboratory Fund—61422150101—AI Navigation Methods for Unmanned Maritime Navigation [重点实验室基金-61422150101-面向水中无人航行器的人工智能方法]," *Whole Military Weapons and Equipment Purchase Information Net* [全军武器装备采购信息网], May 19, 2017.

"Major Laboratory Fund—61423011001—Distribution and Resource Optimization and Path Planning for Multiple Drone Cooperative Missions [重点实验室基金-61423011001-异构多无人机协同任务分配、资源优化和路径规划系统]," *Whole Military Weapons and Equipment Purchase Information Net* [全军武器装备采购信息网], May 19, 2017.

Mianzi Jingxuan, "Are They Approaching Hell? China Will Implement Black Mirror's Scoring System [他人即地狱？中国要实行《黑镜》里的评分制了]," *Sohu*, December 14, 2017. As of October 1, 2018:
https://www.sohu.com/a/210521464_630175

MIIT—*See* Ministry of Industry and Information Technology.

Ministry of Education, "Ministry of Education Issues and Distributes the Artificial Intelligence Innovation Action Plan for Colleges and Universities [教育部印发《高等学校人工智能创新行动计划," April 15, 2018.

Ministry of Industry and Information Technology, "Ministry of Industry and Information Technology Big Data Industry Development Plan (2016–2020) [工业和信息化部关于印发大数据产业发展规划（2016－2020年）]," December 18, 2016.

Ministry of Public Security, "Big Data Thinking Improves Police Innovation in Weifang, Shandong [山东潍坊大数据思维推进治安防控创新升级]," September 22, 2015a. As of May 7, 2018:
http://www.mps.gov.cn/n2255079/n4876594/n4974590/n4974592/n5116769/n5116879/c5128612/content.html

———, "Establishing the Big Data Public Security Concept [建立大数据公共安全理念]," September 28, 2015b. As of May 7, 2018:
http://www.mps.gov.cn/n2255079/n4876594/n4974590/n4974592/n5116769/n5116878/c5128484/content.html

———, "Weifang, Shandong, Uses Big Data to Innovate a 3-D Law Enforcement System [山东潍坊运用大数据思维创新立体治安防控体系]," October 7, 2015c. As of May 7, 2018:
http://www.mps.gov.cn/n2255079/n4876594/n4974590/n4974592/n5116769/n5116879/c5128660/content.html

———, "Hangzhou, Jiangsu, Creates a Revolution in Public Security by Researching a Convenient App [浙江杭州警方研发便民服务APP 用大数据助力公安改革]," May 2, 2016. As of May 7, 2018:
http://www.mps.gov.cn/n2255079/n4242954/n4841045/n4841079/c5285368/content.html

———, "Online P2P Is Even Harder to Govern Than Internet Fraud! Xiamen Anti-Fraud Center Develops New Tool to Manage It [比电信诈骗更难治理的是网贷P2P! 厦门市继反诈中心又出大数据监管利器]," January 12, 2017a. As of May 7, 2018:
http://www.mps.gov.cn/n2255079/n5590589/n5596621/n5596632/c5599762/content.html

———, "Explanation of the State Council's Guidance Opinions on the Anti–Money Laundering, Anti–Terror Funding, Anti–Tax Evasion System [《国务院办公厅关于完善反洗钱、反恐怖融资、反逃税监管体制机制的意见》政策解读]," September 29, 2017b.

———, "Press Conference on the State Council's Guidance Opinions on the Anti–Money Laundering, Anti–Terror Funding, Anti–Tax Evasion System [《国务院办公厅关于完善反洗钱、反恐怖融资、反逃税监管体制机制的意见》答记者问]," September 29, 2017c.

———, "Publication of the State Council's Guidance Opinions on the Anti–Money Laundering, Anti–Terror Funding, Anti–Tax Evasion System [国务院办公厅关于完善反洗钱、反恐怖融资、反逃税监管体制机制的意见》正式印发]," September 29, 2017d.

Moon, Grace, "This Is How South Korea Flattened Its Coronavirus Curve," NBC News, March 24, 2020. As of March 26, 2020: https://www.nbcnews.com/news/world/how-south-korea-flattened-its-coronavirus-curve-n1167376

Mozur, Paul, "Inside China's Dystopian Dreams: A.I., Shame and Lots of Cameras," *New York Times*, July 8, 2018.

———, "Internet Users in China Expect to Be Tracked. Now, They Want Privacy," *New York Times*, January 4, 2018.

Mozur, Paul, Raymong Zhong, and Aaron Krolik, "In Coronavirus Fight, China Gives Citizens a Color Code, with Red Flags," *New York Times*, March 1, 2020.

MPS—*See* Ministry of Public Security.

National Development and Reform Commission, "Main Functions of the NDRC," undated.

———, "List of 2018 Internet+, AI, and Digital Economy Experiments Major Projects Recipients [2018年"互联网+"、人工智能创新发展和数字经济试点重大工程拟支持项目名单公示]," December 27, 2017.

National Information Security Standardization Technical Committee, ["国家标准GB/T 35273-2017 《信息安全技术 个人信息安全规范》获批发布"], January 24, 2018.

"Naval Advanced Research—Ship Big Data Mining and Processing Technology [海军预研-船舶大数据挖掘与处理技术]," *Whole Military Weapons and Equipment Purchase Information Net* [全军武器装备采购信息网], August 14, 2016.

"Naval Innovation—30201050110—Marine Remote Sensing Target Information Mining Technology Based on Deep Learning [海军创新-30201050110-基于深度学习的海洋遥感目标信息挖掘技术]," *Whole Military Weapons and Equipment Purchase Information Net* [全军武器装备采购信息网], March 31, 2017.

"Naval Innovation—30201050111—Image Processing and Ship Target Recognition Based on Artificial Intelligence [海军创新-30201050111-基于人工智能的图像处理和舰船目标识别技术]," *Whole Military Weapons and Equipment Purchase Information Net* [全军武器装备采购信息网], March 31, 2017.

"Naval Innovation—30201050404—Technology to Provide Information on Targets in the Middle and Far Seas with Big Data [海军创新-30201050404-基于大数据的中远海海上目标信息处理技术]," *Whole Military Weapons and Equipment Purchase Information Net* [全军武器装备采购信息网], April 25, 2017.

"Naval Innovation—30202021401—Underwater Sound Detection and Recognition Based on Big Data [海军创新-30202021401-基于大数据的水声探测与识别技术]," *Whole Military Weapons and Equipment Purchase Information Net* [全军武器装备采购信息网], March 31, 2017.

"Naval Innovation—30205020708—Intelligent Control Technology for Construction Process Based on Big Data Analysis [海军创新-30205020708-基于大数据分析的建造过程智能管控技术]," *Whole Military Weapons and Equipment Purchase Information Net* [全军武器装备采购信息网], March 31, 2017.

"Naval Research: Satellite Data Mining Technology Based on Big Data [海军预研-基于大数据的卫星信息数据挖掘技术]," *Whole Military Weapons and Equipment Purchase Information Net* [全军武器装备采购信息网], August 1, 2016.

Navdeep, Preet, Manish Arora, and Neeraj Sharma, "Role of Big Data Analytics in Analyzing e-Governance Projects," *Gian Jyoti e-Journal*, Vol. 6, No. 2, April–June 2016, pp. 53–63.

NDRC—*See* National Development and Reform Commission.

"New Generation Artificial Intelligence Development Plan [新一代人工智能发展规划]," State Council, July 20, 2017.

"Planning Outline for the Construction of a Social Credit System (2014–2020)," *China Copyright and Media*, blog post, June 14, 2014, updated April 25, 2015. As of October 11, 2018:
https://chinacopyrightandmedia.wordpress.com/2014/06/14/planning-outline-for-the-construction-of-a-social-credit-system-2014-2020/

Pollpeter, Kevin L., Michael S. Chase, and Eric Heginbotham, *The Creation of the PLA Strategic Support Force and Its Implications for Chinese Military Space Operations*, Santa Monica, Calif.: RAND Corporation, RR-2058-AF, 2017. As of October 12, 2018:
https://www.rand.org/pubs/research_reports/RR2058.html

"Production Process Simulation and Control System Based on Big Data [基于大数据的生产过程仿真和控制系统]," *Whole Military Weapons and Equipment Purchase Information Net* [全军武器装备采购信息网], November 22, 2016.

"Public Security Police Cloud Infrastructure Construction and Design [公安警务云基础建设方案设计]," *Journal of People's Public Security University of China (Science and Technology)* [中国人民公安大学警务信息工程学院], January 2016.

Ramzy, Austin, and Chris Buckley, "'Absolutely No Mercy': Leaked Files Expose How China Organized Mass Detentions of Muslims," *New York Times*, November 16, 2019.

Sayler, Kelley M., *Artificial Intelligence and National Security*, Washington, D.C.: Congressional Research Service, R45178, updated November 21, 2019. As of October 11, 2018:
https://fas.org/sgp/crs/natsec/R45178.pdf

"Secretary of the Public Security Bureau of Luzhou Wang Lujun Visited Li County [巴州公安局王鲁军局长到焉耆县调研]," May 17, 2017.

Singh, Abhijit, "Is China Really Building Missiles with Artificial Intelligence?" *The Diplomat*, September 21, 2016. As of October 12, 2018: https://thediplomat.com/2016/09/ is-china-really-building-missiles-with-artificial-intelligence/

"Space Flight System Modeling Major Laboratory Fund—6142002302— Autonomous Systems to Identify Optimal Paths to Victory Based on Shifting Situations [航天系统仿真重点实验室基金—6142002302—基于事件演化的智能化制胜规则寻优方法]," *Whole Military Weapons and Equipment Purchase Information Net* [全军武器装备采购信息网], November 25, 2018.

State Council, "Action Plan for Promoting the Development of Big Data [促进大数据发展行动纲要]," August 31, 2015.

State Council, "Internet Financial Risk Improvement Special Implementation Plan [互联网金融风险专项整治工作实施方案]," December 4, 2016a. As of May 7, 2018: http://www.gov.cn/zhengce/content/2016-10/13/content_5118471.htm

State Council, "State Council Guidance Principles for the Building of the Social Credit System [国务院办公厅关于加强个人诚信体系建设的指导意见]," December 30, 2016b. As of May 8, 2018: http://www.gov.cn/zhengce/content/2016-12/30/content_5154830.htm

State Council, "Plan for Developing a New Generation of AI [新一代人工智能发展规划]," July 8, 2017. As of May 20, 2018: http://www.gov.cn/zhengce/content/2017-07/20/content_5211996.htm

Tan Shaoying [谈少盈], Li Xiaoping [李小平], and Wang Pinpin [王品品], "Practice of the U.S. Military's Using Big Data for Promoting Military Vocational Education and Their Enlightenments [美军运用大数据促进军事职业教育的做法及启示]," *Journal of the Air Force Early Warning Academy* [空军预警学院学报], Vol. 4, 2016.

"Using Big Data and Machine Learning to Analyze and Forecast from Multiple Information Sources-315020301 [信息系统-315020301-大数据背景下基于深度学习的多源情报分析与预测技术]," *Whole Military Weapons and Equipment Purchase Information Net* [全军武器装备采购信息网], August 28, 2016.

Wang Feiyue [王飞跃], "The Coming Revolution in National Defense Weaponry and Systems: From 3-D Printing to Parallel Military Systems [国防装备与系统的未来变革:从3D打印到平行军事体系]," *National Defense Science and Technology* [国防科技], Vol. 3, 2013.

Wang Jincheng, "Technological Guidance to Service Actual Combat, Strongly Promoting the Construction and Application of Big Data Policing Cloud Computing Across the Entire Force [王金城——科技引导 服务实战强力推进大数据警务云计算全警建设应用]," *Police Technology*, March 2015. As of May 4, 2018:
http://jcjs.ijournal.cn/ch/reader/create_pdf.aspx?file_no=20150306&flag=1&journal_id=jcjs&year_id=2015

Wang Junping [王君平], and Luo Guojin [罗国金], "China's First Medical Big Data Applied Technology Laboratory Established at the PLA General Hospital [国内首家医疗大数据应用技术国家工程实验室在解放军总医院成立]," *People's Daily*, November 26, 2017.

Wang Pingli [王萍丽], Wu Zheng [吴政], and Wu Yinghao [吴英昊], "Researching Problems of Modern Military Distance Education in an Era of Big Data [大数据时代军队现代远程教育发展问题研究]," *Continuing Education* [继续教育], Vol. 12, 2014.

Wang Shoubiao [王寿彪], Li Xinming [李新明], and Liu Dong [刘东], "Concept Association Mechanisms and Model Structures on Equipment System of Systems with Big Data [大数据与装备体系的概念关联机理和模型结构]," *Journal of the Chinese Academy of Electronics and Information Technology* [中国电子科学研究院学报], Vol. 5, 2016.

Wang Wang [王王], "Based on the Risk of Military Sports Training Under Big Data Management Research [基于大数据下的军事体育训练风险管理初探]," *Journal of Military Physical Education and Sports* [军事体育学报], Vol. 1, 2017.

Webster, Graham, Rogier Creemers, Paul Triolo, and Elsa Kania, "China's Plan to 'Lead' in AI: Purpose, Prospects, and Problems," New America, blog post, August 1, 2017. As of October 12, 2018:
https://www.newamerica.org/cybersecurity-initiative/blog/chinas-plan-lead-ai-purpose-prospects-and-problems/

Xing Jinrong [邢金融], and Zhang Yiming [张一明], "Using Big Data to Improve the Effectiveness of Military HR [运用大数据提升军事人力资源管理效能], *Theoretical Studies on PLA Political Work* [军队政工理论研究], Vol. 5, 2016.

"Yecheng County Public Security Bureau 'Integrated Joint Combat Platform' Second Phase Equipment Project Single Source Procurement Publicity KSYCX (DY) 2017–29 [叶城县公安局"一体化联合作战平台"二期设备项目单一来源采购公示KSYCX（DY）2017-29号]," August 24, 2017.

Yuan, Shawn, "How China Is Using AI and Big Data to Fight the Coronavirus," Al Jazeera, March 1, 2020. As of March 26, 2020:
https://www.aljazeera.com/news/2020/03/china-ai-big-data-combat-coronavirus-outbreak-200301063901951.html

Yuan Yi [袁艺], "Will AI Command Future Wars? [人工智能将指挥未来战争？]," *Defense Daily* [中国国防报], January 12, 2017. As of September 28, 2018: http://www.mod.gov.cn/jmsd/2017-01/12/content_4769771.htm

Zhang Xudong [张旭东], "Zhang Xudong: Seize the Initiative in Future Battlefield Data [张旭东：抢占未来战场数据主导先机]," *Liberation Army Daily*, August 31, 2017. As of May 10, 2018: http://www.71.cn/2017/0831/962728.shtml

Zhao Jiaxin [赵家新], Li Yirui [李沂瑞], and Tian Tingjiang [田廷江], "Shuyang, Jiangsu, Uses Big Data to Make Social Management Smarter [江苏宿迁运用大数据提升社会治理智能度]," Ministry of Public Security, November 28, 2016. As of May 7, 2018: http://www.mps.gov.cn/n2255079/n4876594/n4974590/n5374167/c5556000/content.html

Zheng Liang [郑良], "Fujian Uses Big Data to Solve the People's Problems [福建大数据破解民生痛点]," Ministry of Public Security, January 14, 2017. As of May 7, 2018: http://www.mps.gov.cn/n2255079/n5590589/n5596621/n5596632/c5602218/content.html

Zhong Jun [钟军], "Exploring the Use of Big Data to Innovate the Investigation of the Country's Mobilization Potential [关于利用大数据创新国防动员潜力调查工作模式的探索]," *Information Technology and Informationization* [信息技术与信息化], Vol. 9, 2016.